ENDING OUR RESISTANCE TO LOVE

The Practice of *A Course in Miracles*

ENDING OUR RESISTANCE TO LOVE

The Practice of *A Course in Miracles*

Kenneth Wapnick, Ph.D.

Foundation for A Course in Miracles®

...tion for A Course in Miracles®
41397 Buecking Drive
Temecula, CA 92590

First printing, 2004

Printed in the United States of America

Library of Congress Cataloging in Publication Data

Wapnick, Kenneth
Ending our resistance to love : a practice of a Course in miracles / Kenneth Wapnick.
p. cm.
Includes index.
ISBN 1-59142-132-2
1. Course in miracles. 2. Spiritual life. I. Title.
BP605.C68W3586 2004
299'.93--dc22 2004047181

CONTENTS

Preface

In July of 2003, I went to Atlanta to give a four-day class on "The Journey: From the Ego Self to the True Self," and a weekend workshop on "Living in the World: Prison or Classroom."[1] Before the week of formal classes began, Olivia Scott—my host for the week—asked me to give a two-hour talk for one of her regular classes on *A Course in Miracles*. The group had been going through my book on the four obstacles to peace—*The Journey Home*—and was up to Chapter 11, where I discussed "The Fear of Redemption" from Chapter 13 in the text. Olivia asked if I could address this section, which I did. The session was taped, though so informally that it was not salvageable for public distribution. Yet one of the participants, Sandy Aycock, was able to hear well enough to make a transcript of my talk.

Olivia sent me the transcription, with the suggestion it might be made into a book, and when I read Sandy's excellent and faithful transcription, I agreed. I was impressed with the coherent statement the meeting provided on resistance and its undoing through the process of looking at it with Jesus. Combined with two articles on the same subject that appeared in our

---

1. These recordings have been released on CD and cassette tape.

Foundation's *Lighthouse*, this seemed like a helpful publication on this very important theme that goes to the heart of the practice of *A Course in Miracles*.

The talk has been edited for ease of reading, and some points have been expanded, along with a few passages from *A Course in Miracles* added to supplement the discussion. The informality of the meeting has been retained, however, along with some of the questions that were asked in the course of my talk.

Thus, what you are about to read is a discussion of the important theme of resistance to letting go of one's ego, one of the central blocks to our learning and practicing Jesus' message in *A Course in Miracles*. The articles from *The Lighthouse* elaborate on this theme. The first article, "Resistance: How One Studies *A Course in Miracles* Without Really Learning It," expands on Freud's contribution to the understanding of resistance, with special reference to one's study of *A Course in Miracles*. The second, "The Diver," uses Schiller's wonderful poem of the same name to delve more deeply into the source of our resistance: our fear of looking at the ego's thought system of guilt and hate, behind which is the true resistance of remembering the love of our Self.

Acknowledgements

I should like to thank Olivia Scott, whose gracious hospitality made the Atlanta trip possible, as well as providing the setting for the class on which this book is based. I am grateful, too, to Sandy Aycock whose transcription of the audio tape was the foundation for this book. And finally, to Rosemarie LoSasso, our Foundation's Publications Director, whose preliminary and subsequent editing of the transcript was invaluable in the preparation of the final product.

1. Resistance

I will begin with the major theme of Chapter 11 in my book *The Journey Home*, called "The Fear of Redemption." In that chapter, I speak of our fear of love as a prelude to discussing the "lifting of the veil," which is the subsection of the fourth and final obstacle to peace, "The Fear of God," as well as being the culmination of the discussion on the four obstacles. The section, "The Fear of Redemption" in Chapter 13 of the text, focuses on fear in a way that is different from other places in *A Course in Miracles*. It explains why almost all students of the Course experience the identical problem: Despite their being committed to what *A Course in Miracles* says—devoting months, years, if not a lifetime to it—they still find themselves doing the exact opposite of what Jesus says. They judge, indulge in specialness—whether special hate or special love—and do all the things people not associated with the Course do. The only difference is they feel guilty because they are not doing what they think Jesus is asking them to do. This section, again, zeros in on the problem, for it goes to the heart of the issue of *resistance*.

One of Freud's early insights, which became a cornerstone of his theory and practice of psychoanalysis, arose from the observation that his patients were not getting better. They should have been improving according to what he thought was happening in the sessions, and he did not understand why they were not. One day, as a result of one of his patient's dreams, the reason dawned on him. In the dream the patient was trying to prove him wrong. This did not make sense to Freud at first. Why would his patient try to prove him wrong when she was paying him a great deal of money and doing a lot of hard work? Nonetheless, she wanted to prove him wrong. Suddenly it occurred to Freud that deep down, she, as well his other patients did not *want* to get well. They wanted to keep their neuroses and their problems. That is when he first understood the concept of *resistance*.

Jesus alludes to this over and over again in *A Course in Miracles*. He does not always use the term *resistance*—most of the time he does not—but he does talk about there being a part of us that does not want to learn his Course. As an example, at the beginning of Lesson 185, "I want the peace of God," he says: "To say these words is nothing. But to mean these words is everything" (W-pI.185.1:1-2). Everyone would *say* they want the peace of God, even if they are atheists. Everyone wants the peace that St. Paul says surpasses all understanding (Philippians 4:7), the peace that allows us to be totally unaffected by what happens around us, whether from the world-at-large or our personal worlds. Regardless of what occurs, we all want the experience of being calm, peaceful, and loving. Yet it seems we do everything to bring about the exact opposite. We are studying a book that promises us that if we study it, identify with its thought system, and put it into practice, we will experience the peace of God. And then we find ourselves doing the exact opposite of what it tells us to do. In "The Consistency of Means and End" from the text, as well as other places, Jesus makes it clear that if we do not employ the *means* of forgiveness that he offers us, it is because we do not want the *end*, which is remembering God. The fault lies not, to paraphrase Cassius, in the stars of *A Course in Miracles*, but in ourselves:

> We have said much about discrepancies of means and end, and how these must be brought in line before your holy relationship can bring you only joy. But we have also said the means to meet the Holy Spirit's goal will come from the same Source as does His purpose. Being so simple and direct, this course has nothing in it that is not consistent. The seeming inconsistencies, or parts you find more difficult than others, are merely indications of areas where means and end are still discrepant. And this produces great discomfort. This need not be. This course requires almost nothing of you. It is impossible to imagine one that asks so little, or could offer more (T-20.VII.1).

A Course in Miracles helps us understand that it is not the world or people that cause us to be upset; we *allow* them to upset us. That is where resistance comes in, and that is what is addressed in "The Fear of Redemption." The section is in two parts, the first of which teaches us that our real fear is not of crucifixion, but of redemption—that if we truly experience the Love of God, we will leave this world entirely and leap into our Father's Arms. The second part is more specifically about specialness, even though the word itself is not used. When we demanded special favor from God and He did not give it to us, we changed Him into our own image and likeness:

> You were at peace until you asked for special favor. And God did not give it for the request was alien to Him, and you could not ask this of a Father Who truly loved His Son. Therefore you made of Him an unloving father, demanding of Him what only such a father could give (T-13.III.10:2-4).

In Chapter 16 Jesus returns to this belief that God did not grant us the special love we demanded from Him, and we therefore went out and got it on our own:

> It is in the special relationship, born of the hidden wish for special love from God, that the ego's hatred triumphs. For the special relationship is the renunciation of the Love of God, and

> the attempt to secure for the self the specialness that He denied (T-16.V.4:1-2).

This, then, is the core of the problem: We *believe* this happened, but in reality it never happened at all. At some point in the state of perfect Oneness, in our Identity as God's one Son, the thought emerged—what the Course later refers to as the "tiny, mad idea"—that we could be separate from God. When the thought was taken seriously and experienced as reality, we began to experience ourselves as a separate entity, a distinct personality that could know itself in relation to God. This was the inception of the dream of separation, and was unheard of before. Actually it has always been unheard of because it never really happened—the impossible could simply not occur. Within our dream, of which this world is the ultimate expression, it appeared as if the impossible indeed occurred: we embraced the thought that we have an individual, special, and unique self. That was the beginning of the problem, and its undoing is its ultimate end. Everything in between constitutes our experiences in this world.

These experiences are predicated on our coveting a special, individual existence. We like having a personality. Even though for most of us we have not always been happy and we experience pain and suffering all through our lives—physically and psychologically—

we still cling to this self because it is all we have. The other Self does not exist here. It has no separate identity or personality. It has nothing. It is but part of God's Wholeness and Love.

While few of us, if any, ever get in touch with that original thought of being separate from God, we could certainly get in touch with the thought of a personal self. If you are honest, you recognize there is a part of you that luxuriates in your problems—past hurts, abuse, victimization, abandonment, and betrayal. As painful as these experiences are, they define us and provide our identities. They are what make us who we are as adults. We survived infancy, childhood, and especially adolescence, by developing a self that learned how to adjust to a world that does not always meet our needs and give us what we want. We learned at a very early age how to develop a special self and identity that could cope with and survive the constant sense of threat. That is the self we now cherish and attempt to hold on to, no matter what the cost.

This cherishing of our self-concepts is the underlying premise of this section, "The Fear of Redemption," and it sheds light on why we all have so much trouble with this Course, if we really understand it for what it is. When people do *not* have trouble with it, it is very often because they have rewritten it without realizing they have done so. They believe, for example, that *A Course in Miracles* does not mean *literally* that the world is an illusion and that we will one day leave it. They believe that only our pain is illusory, and if we really practice this Course, Jesus will help us live more happily in the world. That is, after all, what we secretly want. We want to have our ego's cake, eat it, and enjoy it, too! We want to be saved; we want to have an experience of Jesus and of Heaven's Love; but we want it to be in the context of our dreams of separation and specialness. We do not realize that to follow *A Course in Miracles* means stepping outside the dream to where Jesus is, and at the end, awakening from the dream entirely.

What the world has done with Jesus over the centuries, and what we are still trying to do through his Course, is bring him and his message into the dream so that we would be taught how to *keep* our self—but as a happy, peaceful, and fulfilled self. When we finally come to recognize that Jesus is teaching us that that self, too, is an illusion, and that the ultimate purpose of having him as our teacher is so that we would leave the world entirely, the fear and anxiety start to build. That is our fear of redemption. We would much rather live with a God of crucifixion, just as Christianity has done—whether it is a theological God, a personal God, or a God of suffering—rather than let that go and just be with the God Who truly redeems us by His Voice reminding us that nothing happened. That is the fear, and that is where our resistance is lodged—

the final veil of unforgiveness, to use the imagery of the glorious final section of "The Obstacles to Peace" (T-19.IV-D). When we pass through this veil, our self disappears, as Jesus joyously describes:

> Together we will disappear into the Presence beyond the veil, not to be lost but found; not to be seen but known (T-19.IV-D.19:1).

To be known, which in *A Course in Miracles* is Heaven, means there is no self. Thus, when we pass through that final veil with Jesus, we disappear into the Presence of God and the Presence of Christ, our true Self. We are no longer seen as an individual self, for seeing—or perception—is part of the illusory world in which this individual, separated, special self lives.

The prospect of our disappearing leaves us terror-stricken. And Jesus describes what happens as we stand before that final veil:

> And now you stand in terror before what you swore never to look upon. Your eyes look down, remembering your promise to your "friends." The "loveliness" of sin, the delicate appeal of guilt, the "holy" waxen image of death, and the fear of vengeance of the ego you swore in blood not to desert, all rise and bid you not to raise your eyes. For you realize that if you look on this and let the veil be lifted, *they* will be gone forever. All of

> your "friends," your "protectors" and your "home" will vanish. Nothing that you remember now will you remember (T-19.IV-D.6).

Instead of looking through the veil and seeing the Light, then disappearing into it, our eyes look down, remembering our promise to our "friends." What prompts us to lower our eyes is *resistance*: our reaction to the fear of losing our identity, this self. In the following passage from the *Psychotherapy* pamphlet, Jesus treats resistance as the ego's means of protecting itself from true growth, by substituting its own definition, which of course means retaining our special self and having it "grow" in stature and respect. All the while, of course, the only change that has occurred is a deeper identification with the ego's shadows of guilt:

> The patient hopes to learn how to get the changes he wants without changing his self-concept to any significant extent.... The self he sees is his god, and he seeks only to serve it better.... "Resistance" is its [the ego's] way of looking at things; its interpretation of progress and growth. These interpretations will be wrong of necessity, because they are delusional. The changes the ego seeks to make are not really changes. They are but deeper shadows, or perhaps different cloud patterns (P-2.in.3:3,6; I.2:4-7).

As we steadfastly make our way closer and closer to that choice point, our fear and anxiety intensify. There is a little voice within, not the still, small voice of the Holy Spirit, but the still, small voice of the ego—except it does not seem very small and is not very still—that screams in our ear and says: "Remember what I told you? Take one more step with this Jesus fellow, take one more step on this forgiveness path, take one more step toward letting go of your past and your grievances, and you will disappear. But not into the Heart of God. You will disappear into the bowels of oblivion. You will be annihilated." That is when fear erupts and our eyes look down, and we remember our promise to our friends. Sickness appears; anger, grievances, past hurts, and fantasies of specialness rise in our consciousness. All the things that have saved us in the past now rise up and come to our "rescue."

It is very helpful to be aware of this so that when it happens, as it inevitably will, you would not feel guilty or upset. You would simply say: "This is what the book said would happen and what Jesus said would happen. Therefore, I should not be surprised now that it is happening, and above all I should not feel guilty. After all, I have a split mind. There is the right-minded side of me that yearns to return home, that has committed itself to this Course and is working diligently with it, studying and above all practicing it.

But there is also the wrong-minded side of me that still identifies with my ego and with my special, individual self. I should not be surprised when every once in a while that wrong-minded self rears its ugly head and begins whispering its sweet nothings about anger and grievances, fear and hate, loss and pain." You learn to respond to your ego with: "Oh yes, of course, that is what this is. I know who you are, and I no longer have to be afraid of you or feel guilty." Learning not to be afraid of the ego is what causes it gradually to disappear.

What also helps as you continue on your journey is remembering that you do not lose your self immediately. You begin by substituting a happier self for an unhappy one. You learn to become more joyful, peaceful, kind, and gentle; less angry, anxious, fearful, and depressed. Those are the happy dreams *A Course in Miracles* talks about. But that just gets you half-way up the ladder; it is not the ultimate goal. The real goal is to get you to the top, which is the real world. What gets you there is recognizing that even the happy dream is a dream; even this figure in the happy dream is illusory. Even though I am less angry and anxious than before, more peaceful and kind, I am not yet identified with the peace of God. These are the important steppingstones towards achieving that peace; but it is not the ultimate peace. That is why there are *four* obstacles to peace. The fourth and final obstacle is the penetration of the final veil, which in the end is not even a penetration. The veil just dissolves. But you must recognize the fear that builds up as you get closer and closer to that final veil, and to your resistance to passing beyond it. You begin to have intimations that *A Course in Miracles* is saying more than you thought it was. This is not a journey to a happier dream. This is a journey *home*.

2. Looking at Resistance

Q: Once you meet the resistance, do you just stay with it?

A: Yes, once you meet with the resistance, you become as fully aware of it as you can. Freud said that one of the key elements in successful treatment is to have the person become more aware of the resistance. The similarities between Freud and *A Course in Miracles* are striking, both in theory and in practice. All you need do is become aware of the resistance and say: "Oh, there I go again. Obviously I have a split mind. What else is new?" In a sense, that attitude of indifference and nonchalance will enable you finally to get past it.

The worst thing you can do, and the last thing you want to do, is fight against your fear. Don't resist the resistance; simply be aware of it. In "Rules for Decision" in Chapter 30, under the very first rule Jesus says: "*Do not fight yourself*" (T-30.I.1:7). Do not fight against your fear. Do not fight against the ego. When you do, you make it real. There is a wonderful line in the Bible: "Resist not evil" (Matthew 5:39). From the perspective of *A Course in Miracles*, when you resist evil you have made it real, and therefore even stronger. When you fight aggression with aggression, or attack with attack—whether you do it personally or as a head of state—you will never have peace. Never. That is why there will never be peace in the Middle East, Africa, the Indian subcontinent, or anywhere else. It is always hate fighting hate, aggression fighting aggression, with both sides of every conflict convinced they are justified in what they are doing. The thought system of hate—which ultimately is the thought system of separation and attack—is repeatedly reinforced. How can you possibly undo something you are continually strengthening? The way to weaken it is to step back and observe it. Reacting makes it real; gently observing it undoes it. There is a crucial section at the end of Chapter 23 called "Above the Battleground," which comes shortly after "The Laws of Chaos," the heart and soul of the Course's treatment of the ego system. Being above the battleground means raising yourself beyond the body—not literally, of course—to be with Jesus *in your mind*, looking back down on the battleground of specialness and bodies in the world. You observe the battleground and do nothing more.

Two lines I frequently quote are illustrative of this process. One has to do with forgiveness, and the other with the miracle, which are virtually identical. Both statements are in the workbook in Part II. In the summary on forgiveness Jesus states that forgiveness "is still, and quietly does nothing.... It merely looks, and waits, and judges not" (W-pII.1.4:1,3). That is a wonderful description that encapsulates the essence of *A Course in Miracles*. The waiting is my patience in not being so afraid. I look at the resistance and do nothing about it. I do not judge it, but merely look.

The same idea is expressed in the summary on the miracle, where Jesus says the miracle "looks on devastation, and reminds the mind that what it sees is false" (W-pII.13.1:3). That is another wonderful description: *The miracle looks on devastation.* It does not look on love, light, or peace. It does not look on Christ or Heaven. It looks on devastation, which has two levels: First, the devastation in the world—the pain and suffering that goes on both internationally and personally. That level comes from the projection of the devastation in our minds, which is the second level. Our minds are tortured with guilt, not to mention with the fear that God will destroy us because we destroyed Heaven. The miracle looks on that devastation and does nothing. It is simply the reminder in our minds that what we are looking at is false. It is the choice of the decision-making part of our minds to join with the Holy Spirit in the forgiving miracle of quietly looking without judgment.

The miracle, or forgiveness, looks on the resistance; it looks on our identification with our self; on our fear of love and forgiveness; our hate, pettiness, selfishness, anger, depression, and scripts of victimization. It looks on all of that, and stops. It "looks, and waits, and judges not." It looks and reminds us that none of this has had any effect on reality. Our resistance to God's Love has not changed Him. Our resistance to awakening to our true Self has not changed It. Nothing has happened.

The *guilt* over our resistance is the problem. The guilt over our decision to leave love, whether we did it ontologically at the beginning, or are doing it here right now is the problem. *A Course in Miracles* tells us that guilt makes us blind and insane:

> Guilt makes you blind, for while you see one spot of guilt within you, you will not see the light. And by projecting it the world seems dark, and shrouded in your guilt. You throw a dark veil over it, and cannot see it because you cannot look within (T-13.IX.7:1-3).

> For you must learn that guilt is always totally insane, and has no reason (T-13.X.6:3).

Guilt says that you have sinned. You have separated from love and therefore are a sinner who deserves to be punished. But if you step back with Jesus and look at what is going on in your mind—which is what it means to have a relationship with him or the Holy Spirit—you end up smiling sweetly and saying: "Isn't that silly!" That is the meaning of his statement at the end of Chapter 27 in the text:

> In gentle laughter does the Holy Spirit perceive the cause, and looks not to effects.... He bids you bring each terrible effect to Him that you may look together on its foolish cause and laugh with Him a while.... And you will leave the holy instant with your laughter and your brother's joined with His (T-27.VIII.9:1,3,8).

This is the gentle laughter that comes from looking at your resistance to the truth; realizing how silly it is to prefer specialness to the Love of God. The next step is to forgive yourself when you feel the need to do something about it; you forgive yourself when you start to feel guilty over resisting love.

Q: What if the resistance comes in the form of pain? You are aware of it and you take medication, which is magic. Is that the same thing?

A: It is exactly the same thing. Of course you take medication if you are in pain, and of course you call up a friend if you are lonely. You do whatever will alleviate your pain. But do not call it salvation. Call it magic, but forgive yourself for using it. After all, doing *anything* in this world is magic. This book, *The Journey Home*, is magic because you believe it has something you do not have. The book that this book talks about, *A Course in Miracles*, is magic. Forgiving yourself for taking magic is the same as forgiving yourself for preferring the magical self of the ego to the true Self of God. If we were totally in our right minds we could heal ourselves just by remembering our Source. But if we could do it that easily, we would not be here. We certainly would not need *A Course in Miracles*. So forgive yourself for thinking you are still a body with needs, and that you still feel bodily pain and pleasure. That does not make you a bad person. It simply makes you insane.

Looking at that without judging yourself or others who may be using magic is the essence of healing. That is how the Holy Spirit would take something whose purpose is to make the ego real—pain, for instance—and turn it around to become an instrument of forgiveness. You can learn to look at your ego choices, to be sick emotionally or physically, and then at your choice to seek magical aid for that illness. You can then learn to remind yourself that those choices have had no effect on reality. You look on the devastation of your choices—the devastation of your magic—and remind yourself that what you are seeing is false and has had no effect on truth.

That is why I continually emphasize there is nothing in *A Course in Miracles* about behavior. There is nothing in this Course that would tell you that something you do or do not do is right or wrong. *A Course in Miracles* is only about changing your mind, which means changing your teacher. When you choose

Jesus—and you will relate to this more and more—you will walk with a gentle smile on your face. Even as you are going through ego experiences, and even though people around you are going through theirs, there will be that gentle smile that does not allow the decision for the ego to become more real than you have already made it. You do not reinforce it. You just look at it. This cannot be said too often.

On the other hand, be vigilant for the temptation to use "looking at your ego with Jesus" as a means of indulging your ego. That is a common temptation. You end up saying: "It's okay if I'm angry with you and hate you, because I'm looking at it with Jesus." "It's okay if I take this knife and stab you, because I'm looking at it with Jesus. At least I know that I am projecting as I push the blade through your heart." Unfortunately, I have heard many of these horror stories, not about people stabbing one another, but about people's distortions about the meaning of *looking with Jesus*. It has become a means of indulging their egos, wherein they are not being honest with themselves in acknowledging how they enjoy their anger and specialness.

Integral to the process of looking with Jesus at your ego is the comparison of the two states: the ego state you are in, and the state you are giving up by choosing the ego. In other words, if I angrily hold grievances against you, I do not experience the peace of God, nor can I experience it if I indulge or luxuriate in my special love relationship with you. It is important to include that step in your processing, because if you do not experience the cost to you of being with your ego, you will not be motivated to give it up. You may become expert at looking with Jesus at your ego, but fifty years from now you will unhappily discover that you are still in your ego. This is inevitable if you have not allowed yourself to feel the searing pain that comes from pushing his love and peace away, and accepting in their place the ego's "shabby substitute" of specialness that *A Course in Miracles* describes (T-16.IV.8:4).

As much as you can, bring both states into your awareness. Contrast the state of the ego's peace, which is spurious, with Jesus' true peace. You will be able to tell which is which, because in Jesus' peace, no one is excluded; everyone is part of it. In the ego's peace, only the good guys, the ones who meet your needs, are allowed in. That is a sure-fire way of telling the difference. Even when you choose the ego—when you love to exclude and hate—you can be aware that you are so insane that you are choosing against the peace of God and telling Jesus that you do not want his love around. If you can at least look at what you are doing and what you are giving up, you would be bringing him in through the back door, because to look without judgment means to look with him. I have said in the past that until you become really nauseated by your ego you will never be motivated to give it up. But that does not mean that you have to become a masochist—the goal is not to be in pain and be sick. Realistically, though, the only thing that will really motivate you to let go of your ego is to be thoroughly sickened by it, becoming fully aware of the pain that results from choosing hate and separation. That is the meaning of these lines that appear early in the text:

> Tolerance for pain may be high, but it is not without limit. Eventually everyone begins to recognize, however dimly, that there *must* be a better way (T-2.III.3:5-6).

Another relevant passage comes at the beginning of "The Happy Learner," where Jesus says that the Holy Spirit needs you to be aware of your misery:

> You who are steadfastly devoted to misery must first recognize that you are miserable and not happy. The Holy Spirit cannot teach without this contrast, for you believe that misery *is* happiness (T-14.II.1:2-3).

What is striking about this is that the section is about the *happy* learner, which means you cannot be a *happy* learner until you first realize how miserable you are. If you are happy, peaceful, and satisfied with your life, *A Course in Miracles* is not for you. There are many other spiritual paths, contemporary ones especially, that would support that. This, however, is a

Course whose purpose is to teach you how miserable you are in this world, identified with the ego's thought system. Otherwise there would be no motivation for you to leave it. If the world works for you, then why would you want to look at your ego? Why would you want to look at your guilt and hate?

You *will* be motivated, however, if you are aware that choosing sickness, separation, and specialness—the principle of *one or the other:* one wins and another loses—makes you anxious and uncomfortable, and brings you pain. Only to the extent that you experience the horror and pain of your decision will you be motivated to say: "There *must* be a better way." This really means: "There must be another teacher in my mind with a different thought system, because the one I am following does not work." As long as you think it works, then *A Course in Miracles* is not for you and you will not need it. You may like it because it says beautiful things beautifully, but you will not be getting from the Course what it is offering, which is a way *out of the dream*, not a way to solidify it.

Q: Once you face this, it seems to me there is a fine line between "ain't it awful" and using this to move on. Could you address that?

A: Everyone wishes there were a precise, detailed formula to follow, but unfortunately there is none, other than to trust that experiencing the pain of staying with your ego will help you get beyond it. That is the bottom line. There are many grizzly passages in *A Course in Miracles* that describe the horror of the ego. It talks about hatred and murder; about throwing your brother off a precipice, of flesh being ripped from bone (T-24.V.4); it talks about "hungry dogs of fear" that "in their savage search for sin... pounce on any living thing they see, and carry it screaming to their master, to be devoured" (T-19.IV-A.12:7; 15:6); it describes the special relationship as a triumph over God (T-16.V.10:1). These are not just empty words. They are deliberately used to help you get in touch with the murderer within.

Reflecting on what it means to be in a body brings this point home even more forcefully (as if that were necessary!). Step back and for a moment and be the proverbial man from Mars. Look at what a body is and how it lives; its life sustained by murder. Think about it—we cannot exist without taking a breath; yet when we do, we devour thousands of microorganisms; we cannot take a step or drive a car without destroying thousands upon thousands of microorganisms, and not just microorganisms, but ants and other insects as well; when we eat, we are devouring something that is not ours, and something that was formerly alive. Whether a potato, turnip, carrot, fish, chicken, or cow, we are eating something that once lived. We do not care! Vegetarians often say they do not want to eat meat or even fish, because they were formerly living organisms. That is true, but so was a carrot. There is no hierarchy of illusions, in contrast to the ego's first law of chaos that there *is*. We usually do not think twice about taking a breath, a step, or eating something, and the purpose here is certainly not to make you feel guilty because you breathe, eat, drink, or move around. But the purpose is to have you realize that the body itself, in which we think we live, is based on murder. You cannot exist without killing something else. In addition, how can we have homes in which to live without the lumber industry chopping down trees?

But as you suggest, you could easily fall into the trap of indulging your ego and luxuriating in it if you say, "ain't it awful," without allowing yourself to *feel* the effects. Your ego should sicken you, as I have repeatedly said. *A Course in Miracles* says "What is not love is murder" (T-23.IV.1:10) and that love is not possible here (T-4.III.4:6). It is pretty terrible when you scratch beneath the surface and discover that beneath this lovely, kind, thoughtful, sensitive, helpful person you think you are, there is a Hitler, a monster who justifies killing on the grounds that it is either kill or be killed! As Freud told his daughter Anna on one of their walks through Vienna:

> You see those lovely houses with their lovely facades? Things are not necessarily so lovely behind the facades. And so it is with human beings too (*Anna Freud: A Biography*, Elizabeth Young-Bruehl [Summit Books, 1988, New York], p. 52).

A mild understatement indeed!

Someone commented earlier about an unsettling self-discovery while working out at the gym. She had recently joined the gym thinking she would be working on her body, only to discover she was really going to work on her ego. The body work, she realized, was only an excuse for changing her ego. She would stand on the treadmill and judge; and all she could see was hate everywhere. She saw her ego in all its horror, dripping with hate and viciousness. It was her mind that was the real gym.

But you must be equally vigilant for the flip side as well: seeing this horrendous content within, and reacting to it as if it were real. The ego is incredibly subtle. If it cannot stop you from studying this Course, it will join you in your study of it. It is an expert at that! Consequently, it is advisable sometimes to have an outside person help you; someone who can reflect to you a balanced way of looking so that you do not get caught on either side. It is very hard to do it by yourself, because the ego is so slippery. Our fear of losing our individual, special self is so intense that we could easily fall into this trap of making the ego real—by rationalizing it or by pushing it down. We need the inner help certainly, but sometimes our ambivalence towards that inner help interferes so much that we then need an outer source of help as well—in any form that would help us walk the path. We would then have an internal *and* external hand to hold on to.

You can keep yourself honest and alert to these ego traps by monitoring your mind for all judgments. If you wake in the morning feeling blissful, thinking you have forgiven everyone, you should be very suspect. If it were that easy, you would not be here—unless you were spiritually advanced, in which case you would not need *A Course in Miracles*. The Course is not for spiritually advanced people; it is for spiritual infants. If you believe you have forgiven everyone, and no longer hold any thoughts of judgment or specialness, the chances are very high you are denying something.

I used to say often when I first started teaching that a good preparation for *A Course in Miracles* is to have already been on a spiritual path and/or to have been through some form of psychotherapy. That at least would have provided a healthy respect for the ego. Students were minimizing the ego in the early years, especially; but it has been happening ever since as well. People do not want to deal with their dark sides, so they wind up saying everything is wonderful: I ask the Holy Spirit's help and He tells me what to order at a restaurant; He forgives everyone for me, and so I love everyone. If your personal experience has given you a healthy respect for your ego, you would be wary of such ploys.

Once again, I think you should be very suspicious of yourself if all of a sudden you wake up one morning in a blissed-out state. It is much, much healthier to wake up consumed with hatred, and then realize you have awakened every other morning consumed with hatred but did not know it. You thought you were feeling love, kindness, or concern. Or maybe you just thought it was a bad day, or indigestion from the meal you had the night before. You did not realize it was hate.

Quite a number of people over the years have said to me, feeling dismayed and disappointed, that the longer they study *A Course in Miracles*, the worse things seem to get in terms of their ego. In general I think that is inevitable. However, the Course helps us realize that things are not really getting worse—*they were already worse*! We simply did not know how horribly bad things were. We were always miserable, but did not know it. *A Course in Miracles*' helpfulness lies in its lifting the veil so we can begin to look inside. The first thing we see, however, is not the Love of God, but the ego's hate—self-hatred, guilt, tension, and anxiety. Before that, we were blissfully going along with our lives. Perhaps we were raising a family, making money, having fun—doing everything normal people do and want to do. We were not aware that all we were involved with was running away from the Love of God, which really means running away from our guilt. Now all of a sudden we realize what our lives are, and we do not like what we are seeing.

In one sense, I would rather hear people tell me that when they work with *A Course in Miracles* things are terrible, rather than that it has changed their lives and everything is absolutely wonderful. When people say things like that, I begin to worry. Not that I am not happy that people are happy, but I would want them to be *truly* happy, rather than be in denial about what is really going on. *A Course in Miracles* undoes such denial. You cannot undo a problem that you do not know you have, as I have been stressing. You have to look at it. And looking at it is very painful, as we read in the text:

> In looking at the special relationship, it is necessary first to realize that it involves a great amount of pain. Anxiety, despair, guilt and attack all enter into it, broken into by periods in which they seem to be gone (T-16.V.1:1-2).

In one sense, that is probably a good sign. Again, you do not want people to be in pain, but if the pain were already there and was just going unnoticed, that is not good, either. In a sense, the cure may seem worse than the problem, but the discomfort is only temporary.

When you are able to begin to smile, you will begin to take the darkness less and less seriously. The light will gradually dawn, and you will start to feel better. But you will not be motivated to take Jesus' hand and look at the darkness until you really feel the pain. That is the point here. This world is an awful place—plain awful. A line in the workbook describes this world as a place "where starved and thirsty creatures come to die" (W-pII.13.5:1). Now that is not a very nice image. We are also told that this world is not our home—we are orphans here (W-pI.182). Even if our Parent were not killed by us, we are not so sure He would welcome us back. We do not even know where back is. *That* is awful! Jesus says at the end of the text that we wander in this world "uncertain, lonely, and in constant fear" (T-31.VIII.7:1) To get in touch with that is hardly pleasant. But that is the only way to get to the love that is just on the other side. In that sense, the process of looking is certainly worth it.

Moreover, *A Course in Miracles* is not meant to make the world a better place, nor to make our lives better in any external way. The Course makes our lives better by helping us realize that there is an inner life—and we do not even have to know what that is at first. All we need know is that the way to get there is to let go of grievances, specialness, and judgments.

Again, it is helpful to become aware of how painful life here really is. Recall the passage we read from "The Happy Learner": the Holy Spirit needs us to recognize how "steadfastly devoted to misery" we are. He cannot teach us unless we recognize that we are miserable and not happy. We have made our miserable existence in this world into a potential for happiness. We believe that the ideal is to be happy and that it can really happen here. But we fail to see that life in this world is really misery, and will never change in form. What changes is the *purpose* we ascribe to our being here: forgiveness instead of judgment, awakening instead of sleep.

In an earlier chapter in the text Jesus tells us that we do not know the difference between pain and joy (T-7.X.8:6), and in the next chapter he says that we do not know the difference between imprisonment and freedom (T-8.II). Again, since we have confused misery and happiness, Jesus has to tell us that we are quite miserable. Essentially he is saying to us: "I know you are miserable because you think you are here in a body that separates you from your Self, everyone else's self, and above all from God. How could you possibly be happy here in a state that is the exact opposite of Heaven, a state of perfect love and peace?" Reflecting Heaven's Oneness in this world is the practical goal of *A Course in Miracles*: to see everyone here as the same. That ends the ego's judgment. If everyone is the same, no one is special. And everyone is the same because we are all equally insane and miserable, but we also are all equally sane.

The idea is to look within and say: "Now I am finally beginning to get a handle on how hateful I am, and how I have identified with my ego." That is a happy learner. Remember—"The Happy Learner" is about learning how miserable you are. One of the operational definitions I give for being in your right mind—which means asking the Holy Spirit or Jesus for help—is being in your wrong mind without judging it. Keep in mind that the happy dream, the right mind, the Holy Spirit, and the Atonement are all *answers* to the ego. They are the *correction* for the ego, and are not anything in and of themselves. The only true positive is the Love of God. What is known as love here is the Holy Spirit's correction for the ego. It cannot have direct expression. Without the ego the Holy Spirit's function of forgiveness disappears, as does He:

> And you will be with him when time is over and no trace remains of dreams of spite in which you dance to death's thin melody. For in its place the hymn to God is heard a little while. And then the Voice is gone, no longer to take form but to return to the eternal formlessness of God (C-6.5:6-8).

Thus, being in the happy dream is being in your wrong mind and having the usual ego attacks, but using them as a way of looking: learning to forgive yourself for having chosen against love, because you chose against love in that original instant. It does not mean waking up and being happy and peaceful. It could mean waking up and being anxious, fearful, guilty, and special, but now seeing this as your classroom. For now at last you know you have a teacher who will properly instruct you. You learn that this is a curriculum *you* wrote, consisting of all your special relationships. You no longer have to deny them, feel guilty, or pretend they are wonderful, and thus are no longer afraid of the pain involved in experiencing them for the guilt-filled things they truly are.

It is helpful to be aware that the process of forgiveness entails going through the darkness, which, by definition, is not pleasant. *A Course in Miracles* tells us that the Holy Spirit will lead you through the circle of fear and that God is on the other side (T-18.IX.3:7-9). But you cannot get to God on the other side unless you go through the circle of fear. I remember an image my wife Gloria once had. She spoke of not being able to get from the world of form to the world of formlessness—that is, God—without crossing the bridge of desolation. Her meaning was clear: you can only reach formlessness by dealing with the desolation of the ego thought system—the bridge that leads you home. It is not pleasant. The great mystic St. John of the Cross originated the evocative phrase "dark night of the soul" that describes the emotionally painful part of the journey home. You do not get to the top of the mountain, which was his image, unless you first climb it—the dark night of looking at one's ego.

A Course in Miracles is very much in accord with this aspect of the spiritual path, teaching that you must go through the ego. At times the process is extremely painful, but what gives you the courage, strength, and hope to prevail is realizing that it is an inevitable part of the process, and above all, that you do not have to go through it alone. That is the value of a relationship with Jesus, our next topic.

3. The Role of Jesus

Crossing this bridge of desolation would be impossible, were it not for the loving and gentle hand to which we cling, that leads us through the clouds of guilt, as Jesus says in the workbook:

> Try to pass the clouds by whatever means appeals to you. If it helps you, think of me holding your hand and leading you. And I assure you this will be no idle fantasy (W-pI.70.9:2-4).

Thus you journey together hand in hand, holding a lamp to search the darkness—and that darkness can be terrifying. We made a world of light—solar and electrical—to illuminate our world, but it is all illusory; an attempt to brighten up a world darkenend by guilt. We do it externally, but it symbolizes our futile attempts to brighten up the inner world of darkness—hate and fear.

Guilt is not wonderful, but what *is* wonderful is that you can bring your thoughts of hatred into the classroom, and have a different teacher interpret them for you. Now you have become a happy learner, because you are truly learning something. There is no point in going to school if you feel you have already learned everything. There is no point in having Jesus as your teacher if you do not think he has anything to teach you. He cannot teach without your special relationships, because they constitute the curriculum. He does not walk into a classroom and lecture you from a textbook. *You* supply him with the teaching material—your life—and he teaches from that. He reads to you from *your* book, and teaches you there is another way of looking at your life and relationships. This approach is going to teach you not how to kill or manipulate the other person, nor how to fix the world; this will teach you how to look at yourself. That is the purpose of being in Jesus' classroom.

When you wake in the morning, realize that you are in class to *un*learn what your ego taught you. It may even be a very difficult classroom this day. Perhaps you have an appointment with a doctor who is going to give you test results that will determine whether you live or die. Or perhaps you will be meeting with your boss at work, and he will tell you that he thinks you are wonderful and deserve a raise, or is going to fire you. Maybe you have a date with a very important person and he or she may love you, or tell you the relationship is over. With your new teacher, no matter what happens, it can be a happy day because of the lessons you will learn.

Q: It is really hard to get in touch with the belief that you murdered God unless you first experience it on the level of the world where you have projected it. If you can really accept that the murderer you see out there is you, then that must also equate to the fact that you really think—below the conscious level—that you have murdered God. And once you face that murderer in you, what do you do with that?

A: Nothing. That is the key, as I have been explaining. What we all did at the beginning as one Son is kill God off because He did not give us what we wanted. We devoured Him psychologically by assuming His creative Self. Believing in horror that we had actually committed what to us was a savagely sinful act (though clearly impossible), we made the non-existent problem of sin real, and became overwhelmed with self-hatred and guilt. The pain of that became so unbearable we had no psychological recourse but to deny the guilt-ridden thing, run away from it, make up a world and body, thereby concealing, not only the guilt, but the mind itself. That is the point.

And so you do not have to get in touch with that original thought of wanting to murder God. It is enough to be aware of how you want to murder the people with whom you live, work, or grew up. It is all the same. That is the beauty of *A Course in Miracles* as a spiritual path. You do not have to deal with God at all; you need only deal with God's representative—your special love or hate partner, past, present, or in the future. This one represents your Father, Whom you see in both a right-minded and a wrong-minded way. The right-minded view of God is that He is the Author of life. The wrong-minded view is that He wants to destroy us. Again, it is not necessary, nor feasible, to deal with any of those thoughts because they are totally buried. But the shadowy fragment of those thoughts is in every one of our relationships:

> What you see as gifts your brother offers [whether it is the gift of thorns: hate and attack, or the gift of lilies: forgiveness] represent the gifts you dream your Father gives to you (T-27.VII.16:2).

To summarize: I do not have to deal with God, only with *you*. If, with Jesus' help, I can undo my specialness with you—my special hate and special love—I am undoing all the interferences between me and God, for they are one. When I complete my path, Jesus happily teaches that the memory of God dawns on my mind and God reaches down and lifts me back unto Himself (see, for example, T-7.I.6-7). Thus, the way I learn to forgive God and love Him is to forgive you.

On an individual level, we get glimpses of this every time we see our egos in action, and then react by saying: "I do not want to look at this." We thus reenact the ontological moment when as one Son we all said: "I do not want to look at this." The body we made up as a defense has eyes that look outward, but not within. Our sensory apparatus was made not to look within the mind, but only to look outward at ours and others' bodies. Why? Because we are terrified of looking at our minds: "Loudly the ego tells you not to look inward, for if you do your eyes will light on sin, and God will strike you blind," as Jesus explains in "The Fear to Look Within" (T-21.IV.2:3). So, accepting the ego's solution to our terror, we made up a world that would never look within at the mind and would deal only with the body—ours and the world's. That is why, incidentally, we invented microscopes and telescopes.

We get to the nitty-gritty of our practical work with *A Course in Miracles* and become aware of the horror of our ego. The temptation is to turn away and run from it. Try not to! That is what a relationship with Jesus is all about. It is not about fixing the dream—winning the lottery, acquiring a relationship or a better body. It is not about anything at all except looking at the ego without fear and without guilt. That is how it is undone, and that is why we need Jesus.

The difficult part of this Course is learning to stay with your ego without falling into the trap of running away from it, indulging it, building an altar to it, or denying it. All Jesus asks us to do is look at it with him, and say: "This really is insane. It is murderous and not loving. Thank God I am beginning to realize I have another choice. But I am also beginning to understand that part of me does not want to make that other choice. If I had *my* way I would stay with the ego, but with less pain." One could say this is a form of self-analysis. You become more and more aware of what the ego is all about. But you stay with it. Otherwise you make it real, and it will remain your identity.

Krishnamurti spoke about staying with the pain. He did not mean it in a masochistic sense, of course, but in the same sense as *A Course in Miracles* when it speaks of pain as a cover for fear, and beyond fear is love. Krishnamurti spoke of going beyond all thought to love. The Course teaches us to stay with the pain of the ego because underneath that is the fear of God's Love. Developing a relationship with Jesus, therefore, means learning not to be so afraid of the pain of your ego that you would run back into the arms of your "friends": hate, sickness, depression, anxiety, specialness. With Jesus always at your side, offering the vision you now accept, fear disappears into the light of truth.

But another layer of resistance can well up at this point: the fear of love. Once you no longer like the way you feel, and no longer want to walk this earth with fear, guilt, and hatred—whether of others or yourself—the question begins to dawn: "What am I really gaining by holding on to this hate? *What will I lose if I let it go*?" That is when the fear of love surfaces very rapidly. We then have second thoughts and begin to retreat: "I don't know if I want that. I don't know if I want to go through a day or even a morning without judging someone. Who would I be if I drove on the highway or joined a gym and no longer judged anyone? Who would I be if I stood on line in the supermarket and no longer judged what was in someone's basket, or the checkout person, or the fact that the sign clearly says ten items or less and this person has thirteen? Who would I be if I stood in the supermarket line and was totally at peace? Who would I be if I drove on the highway and did not attack anyone? Who would I be if I lived with my family and did not have an unkind thought about anyone?"

Becoming aware of these anxieties helps us realize how identified we are with specialness, guilt, judgment, criticism, and hatred. At some point you need to allow yourself to experience how wretched you feel about yourself to walk around with so much judgment. We are so accustomed to judging and finding fault, whether it is something we think is serious and important, or something trivial. It is so much a part of our culture to hate others, especially those judged as different. The problem is we think we are taught to do it, as the song from *South Pacific* expressed. We are *not* taught to do it. We come into the world with it, as well as with the cleverness of how to get away with it—how to make it look as if we are doing something else.

We also come into the world with guilt. It comes in a myriad number of forms, but there is only one guilt, and everyone has it. Thus we are always letting go of the same thing; always dealing with the same issue. The tragic insanity is that we are so identified with that guilt that it is like our DNA. It is not something that can be washed off in the shower. It is woven into our very existence. That is why I made a point of saying earlier that it is helpful to look at the cannibalism of the body. It cannot exist without cannibalizing and murdering everything around us. That is because the ego thought itself is cannibalistic. We all are guilty over that thought—whether it is something mundane or something gargantuan: I was raped in early childhood and that is a huge issue I have to deal with, or I just became furious because a particular person did not say hello to me. It is always all the same.

This is a process because we are dealing with the very roots of our existence. As I was just saying, if we let go of our hate and specialness, we will no longer know who we are. There is a line in "Self-Concept versus Self" that directly addresses this fear:

> There is no statement that the world is more afraid to hear than this:
>
> *I do not know the thing I am, and therefore do not know what I am doing, where I am,*

> *or how to look upon the world or on myself* (T-31.V.17:6).

That is the fear. To us, it is the total negation of our self; but it really is nothing other than the disappearance of a self that never existed in the first place. Again, it does not matter whether I am upset over something trivial or something that has had an enormous impact in my personal life. It is all the same. "A slight twinge of annoyance is nothing but a veil drawn over intense fury" (W-pI.21.2:5). It is a process because its roots are woven into who I believe I am. It would be the same thing as taking a knife and chopping off an arm. That was *my* arm. That is what this feels like. My hatred, my specialness, my self-hatred are who I am. Who would I be without them?

Our lives are defined by the series of defenses we have erected against the self that has been traumatized. Birth is a trauma; being an infant is a trauma; everything is a trauma, because our needs are never totally met as we would want them to be. We spend all our lives dealing with a world that is not there for us—at least not totally, and not all the time. We cope with that pain by erecting defenses, but then the defenses *become* us. It is as if you were to wear the same shirt every single day of your life. After a while it begins to get grafted onto your skin because you never take it off. You can no longer tell where your shirt ends and your skin begins. It becomes who you are. Our defenses are like that. They are like something we put on. Our specialness is not only our mode of operation in the world, but it becomes our identity. That is why the process is so difficult. In reality we are letting go of nothing: it is a journey without a distance (T-8.VI.9:7). Yet in our experience in the world it is everything; it is our very self.

Q: Since this thing that we think we are is all a defense, then there is nothing here except all those layers of defenses.

A: Yes, but this does not mean that you have to get rid of your defenses in order to progress. The value and beauty of having a relationship with Jesus in your mind is that it transcends these defenses entirely. The relationship is not really with a person. The relationship symbolizes your (the decision maker's) choice to identify with a presence in your mind that is still you, but is beyond these layers of defenses. It is part of the process of dis-identifying with the ego thought system of specialness and hate, which is initiated by your choice to look with Jesus at all your ego thoughts.

That is why developing a relationship with Jesus or the Holy Spirit is an intrinsic part of *A Course in Miracles*. You are developing a relationship with the right-minded self that is you, but not the self you thought you were. When you step outside that self and look with Jesus at your ego—at these layers upon layers upon layers—you would no longer feel so helpless and hopeless, and you would understand that there is another self. You do not have to change this self; in fact, you *cannot* change this self, because that is who this body is. But you can step back and look at it from outside that thought system. The more you can do that —day after day, week after week, month after month, year after year—the more you weaken your identification with that self and reinforce your ultimate identification with your true Self.

The principle that allows you to do that is *looking at your ego without judgment*. I cannot say that too often. You look at this self of specialness and say: "My God, I have always been this way. I wanted my mother's and father's love and attention, and I never got enough of it. And then my brother and sister came along, and this one and that one, and all kinds of terrible things happened. I have lived my entire life like that, and I now can see what I am doing in my current family, circle of friends, and with colleagues at work. I see how I am dealing with my body as it gets older, and I see how I react to other bodies in the world and in the news. I see it is all the same."

Thus you look at your ego with Jesus and become aware of the insanity of its thought system, but from outside that thought system. If you could look without guilt, judgment, or fear, you would weaken it significantly. That is the process. All of a sudden you would be filled with hope. There is no hope in this world; there is no hope within the ego's world in your mind. Hate is hate. Dress it up however you will: hate is hate; terror is terror; guilt is guilt. It never changes—it changes form, but its essence never changes. But you do not have to change it, because there is now a position outside it, above the battleground, from which you can look back down and say: "Yes, insanity is all it is."

Q: In asking Jesus for help, I am aware that I am asking him only because I want relief from my pain.

A: What is wrong with that? Why else would you ask him for help? You do not love him. No one who comes to this world loves him. Jesus is not proud; he will get you anyway he can. He knows that the only way he can get you is by helping you feel better, because the pain is so great. At one point, sounding like a learning theorist, he says that he is teaching you to associate pain with the ego, and happiness with letting it go:

> How can you teach someone the value of something he has deliberately thrown away? He must have thrown it away because he did not value it. You can only show him how miserable he is without it, and slowly bring it nearer so he

> can learn how his misery lessens as he approaches it. This teaches him to associate his misery with its absence, and the opposite of misery with its presence. It gradually becomes desirable as he changes his mind about its worth. I am teaching you to associate misery with the ego and joy with the spirit. You have taught yourself the opposite. You are still free to choose, but can you really want the rewards of the ego in the presence of the rewards of God? (T-4.VI.5)

That is how to distinguish between punishment and reward. As psychologists confirmed during decades of research, an animal will learn much more quickly when it is rewarded rather than punished. We do learn through punishment, but not nearly as well as through rewards. Thus Jesus is teaching us to associate punishment with the ego and rewards with him. The only reason we would ask him for help is that we feel better when we do. Our pain lessens when we ask his help to look at a relationship differently. Do not delude yourself into thinking you are asking Jesus for help because you love him. If you really loved him you would not have to ask him for help. Turning away from his love is the source of your guilt, which is the source of your being here. You are not going to know truly what loving him means until the ego is gone.

Another way to express this is to say that you cannot love someone you perceive as different from you. Following the laws of chaos, I must believe that if someone is different from me it is because that person has what I lack, and must have gotten it by stealing it from me. In the Western world, Jesus is the greatest symbol of having what we do not have. He has God's Love; we do not. St. Paul was very clear about that in teaching that we are second-class citizens, the adopted sons of God (Galatians 4:5; Ephesians 1:5); whereas Jesus is first class, the only beloved of his Father. Any child of a family who is not the first-born knows about that. Not only is Jesus God's only beloved Son, he is innocent and totally good. But our egos would have us conclude that he stole that innocence and goodness from us; and therefore he deserved what he got on Calvary. That is our insane "reasoning," the embodiment of the laws of chaos. Jesus specifically refers to this insanity of projecting our seeming sins onto him, and then punishing him for them. That is why he needs us to forgive him, without which we will not be able to accept his help:

> I am made welcome in the state of grace, which means you have at last forgiven me. For I became the symbol of your sin, and so I had to die instead of you. To the ego sin means death, and so atonement is achieved through murder. Salvation is looked upon as a way by which the

> Son of God was killed instead of you.... Let me be to you the symbol of the end of guilt, and look upon your brother as you would look on me. Forgive me all the sins you think the Son of God committed. And in the light of your forgiveness he will remember who he is, and forget what never was. I ask for your forgiveness, for if you are guilty, so must I be. But if I surmounted guilt and overcame the world, you were with me. Would you see in me the symbol of guilt or of the end of guilt, remembering that what I signify to you you see within yourself? (T-19.IV-A.17:1-4; IV-B.6)

As long as you perceive Jesus as different from you—as we all obviously do—you cannot love him. You cannot love anyone in this world who you believe is different from you in a way you have judged to be significant. Therefore, of course you are going to ask Jesus to help you, not because you love him, but perhaps because you *want* to love him. You are aware that you cannot love him and certainly cannot experience his love as long as you are harboring hatred and grievances. But the pain of the hatred and grievance, and the pain of being without his love would motivate you to ask him to help you look at the obstacles to that love: the different forms of specialness. As we were saying earlier, together with Jesus you hold the lamp and go forth to look not at Heaven's bliss, but into the bowels of hell, the cesspool of your ego thoughts. Of such looking is the Course's kingdom on earth, the way of our return to the Kingdom of Heaven.

4. The Role of *A Course in Miracles*

It is important to note that the ego never changes. It is 100% hate and murder. On the other side, the Holy Spirit is 100% love. He never changes. His thought system of forgiveness, healing, peace, and love never changes. Both are totally present in everyone: 100% hate, 100% love. It does not diminish; you do not chip away at it. What changes is the amount of time you spend on either side. It is a mistake to think you can whittle away at your hate. You will never whittle away your hate. It is 100%—like solid granite. There is no tool powerful enough to do anything with that 100% granite wall of hate and murder. What you do is choose to spend less and less time identifying with it, and more and more time identifying with the Correction, the Holy Spirit. That is the meaning of progress in this Course. Therefore, being identified with the Holy Spirit means looking at the ego without judgment. After a while you will realize, as *A Course in Miracles* says, that the solid wall of granite is not solid—it is a thin veil that has no power to block the light. Our perception changes, but the ego does not change: hate is hate; murder is murder. The separation from God was an act of celestial homicide: We believe we destroyed God, and this world arose from His ashes. That is the bottom line. What changes is not the ego; what changes is our perception of it. Our perception will gradually change as we learn to take it less and less seriously, which means we learn to give it less and less power over us. For it is only our minds' belief in the ego that gave it its power:

> *Do not be afraid of the ego.* It depends on your mind, and as you made it by believing in it, so you can dispel it by withdrawing belief from it (T-7.VIII.5:1-2).

The goal of *A Course in Miracles* is not that we be without an ego. The goal is that we not feel guilty about our decision against the Holy Spirit and for the ego.

There is a most important line in the manual that says, "Do not despair, then, because of limitations. It is your function to escape from them, but not to be without them" (M-26.4:1-2). Jesus says the same thing in the section on "The Little Willingness" in the text:

> Trust not your good intentions. They are not enough. But trust implicitly your willingness, whatever else may enter. Concentrate only on this, and be not disturbed that shadows surround it. That is why you came. If you could come without them you would not need the holy instant (T-18.IV.2:1-6).

He is saying that your function is not to be perfect, not to be without the shadows of hate and guilt. Your function is to escape from the burden of guilt you placed upon yourself. It is a very important distinction. "Your function is to escape from them, but not to be without them." In this world, in this dream, you are not expected to be without your guilt, hatred, or murderous impulses, but rather to escape from the burden of judgment you placed upon them.

We are all upset by the original shadow, which is that we deprived ourselves of the Light of God. That is what a shadow is: the deprivation of light. We then felt overwhelmed with guilt, ran away and hid in the world, taking the guilt with us without knowing we had done so. That is why we came: because of the shadows. But we can learn—which is what *A Course in Miracles* helps us to do—not to be upset by the shadows. We can learn not to be upset by our hatred, specialness, and judgments. That is what begins to tip the balance so that we can spend more time with Jesus and less time with the ego.

Q: I feel myself wanting the love so much. But I feel so much fear about accepting it and my true Identity that I just settle back into the ego rather than pushing through to the love. I go back and forth. Can you address how to accept Jesus' help? I do not seem to reach his way.

A: Being aware of that is half the battle. The next half is learning to look at that in yourself without feeling guilty, trying to fix it, or trying to do anything about it. Jesus does not do it for you, but he helps *you* not do anything about it. To be aware that despite whatever issues and problems you have, your real underlying fear is that you do not want to be in the presence of that love, is very useful information. If people truly wanted to be in the presence of love, there would not be a world. There would be no need for *A Course in Miracles*. What gets you into trouble is feeling guilty about it and accusing yourself of betraying Jesus or betraying love, instead of just saying: "Yes, of course, I am afraid of that love. I like being me." To be able to look at your decision to push love away because you are afraid of it without judging yourself is all you ever have to do. Be patient, gentle, and kind with yourself. That is what "The Fear of Redemption" tells us: "You are not really afraid of crucifixion. Your real terror is of redemption" (T-13.III.1:10-11). That is a wonderful section in terms of describing our fear of God's Love. In God's Love, no one exists. There *is* no one. That is why we fear It.

You do not have to confront that fear. All you need do is gradually allow more and more people to come into your life—not physically or externally—but in your *mind*, without judgment. And that includes yourself. Be aware of how you want to exclude certain people. Even if you have not experienced that in your life, look at a movie, or watch the latest news. Every one has a point of view about Iraq, Israel and Palestine, India, Pakistan, and Kashmir, Latin America, or Africa. Every one has a point of view about something in the world or about American politics. Watch the news and see how your buttons get pushed. You will hate and judge some people, and perceive others as the "good guys." That is enough. Do not judge yourself for doing that, but be aware that you are saying there are certain members of the Sonship that you would just as soon not have here. This does not mean you have to agree with everyone, or that you cannot have a political, social, or economic point of view. But when your point of view starts to exclude others, and you feel personal antipathy toward certain people or groups, that should indicate you are still afraid of God's Love.

In God's Love there are no differences. You do not have to know what the Oneness of Heaven is like. In fact, at one point in Chapter 25 Jesus says, "for while you think that part of you is separate, the concept of a Oneness joined as One is meaningless" (T-25.I.7:1). No one really has a clue as to what the concept of "a Oneness joined as One" is. It sounds nice but it really means nothing to us. We do not therefore have to know its meaning, but we can learn that perceptions of differences are never justified. We all are superficially different—race, religion, national origin, gender, age, size, etc.—but these differences do not make a difference. We are all born of the same insane ego, which is the defense against knowing we are part of the one God. It is one of *A Course in Miracles*' central themes that we are all the same in having a wrong mind and a right mind. Everyone's wrong mind is the same; everyone's right mind is the same; and everyone has the same power to choose between them. Everything else is an illusion. In the end, the split mind is an illusion, too. Everything else in this world, as a perception, is unfounded and unjustified. Again, watch how you want to exclude certain people, and then look at that without judgment.

The resistance to this will be enormous, however. As long as you experience yourself as being here, and are sure the image you see in the bathroom mirror every morning is you—even though you may not like what you see—it is insane to think that you will believe that everyone is the same. As long as you identify with your body, you must also identify with the thought system that made that body; a thought system of judgment, specialness, hate, and above all, of separation. So if you are watching a newscast and are totally at peace and feel you love everyone, you should gently say to yourself: "I am a liar."

Allow yourself to have judgments. Allow yourself to watch the latest news from Washington, and then have a definite judgment about what you hear. Allow yourself to be totally invested in your point of view—that yours alone is valid, and that anyone who does not agree with you is clearly mistaken. Then look at that judgment—which is where Jesus comes in—without judging yourself. You are much better off beginning with the assumption that you are a heartless, cruel, sadistic beast, than you are assuming that you are a holy child of God who loves everyone. You are much, much better off beginning with the idea that if you are in this body you are a murderer. Not only are you a murderer, you were a murderer, and will always be a murderer, because you like to be right. You like to exist. You like being a body.

At the beginning of *A Course in Miracles* Jesus says this Course will not teach you the meaning of love, because love cannot be taught. This is a Course in helping you remove the blocks to the awareness of love's presence (T-in.1:6-7). Over and over again he says this is a Course in *undoing*. The Atonement, correction, salvation, the miracle, forgiveness—all undo. The ego speaks first and is always wrong; the Holy Spirit is the Answer. There cannot be an answer unless a problem is first recognized. Answers solve problems. What good is the answer if the problem is unknown? The early workbook lessons are very clear about that. *A Course in Miracles* helps us identify the problem, which we bring to the answer; bringing the illusion to the truth, the darkness to the light. How can we bring the darkness, illusion, and problem to the light, truth, and answer if we do not know we have a problem, let alone where it is?

Before we can experience the love and the peace of the answer, we first have to understand and experience the pain and the ugliness of the problem, which is the hatred. Therefore, we need to give ourselves permission to hate, judge, find fault, and criticize, to have a life of specialness filled with special love and special hate partners. Do not do anything more. Just look at the problem. That is what Jesus tells us: "Together we have the lamp that will dispel [the darkness]" (T-11.V.1:3). *Together.* He cannot do it, and I cannot do it; but my asking him to help me is the lamp that looks at the ego's darkness. Once again it is the *process of looking* at the ego's darkness that dispels it. That is the message and practice of *A Course in Miracles*, and is Jesus' answer to our call for love, an answer that gently undoes our resistance to it.

5. Conclusion

As a closing I will read the poem "Bright Stranger" from *The Gifts of God.* This is one of the poems that reflects Helen's love-hate relationship with Jesus, here more love-fear. She describes how she tries to shut him out, fearful of his love. That is why I discuss this poem in the chapter, "The Fear of Redemption," in *The Journey Home.* Helen's ambivalence with Jesus is indeed reflective of all our relationships and, specifically, our relationship with him: the love, hate, and fear that if we listen to his voice, take his hand, and let his love into our hearts, everything will change. The only way to protect this self from any meaningful change is to protect ourselves against him. Thus our resistance to forgiveness is reflected in our resistance to *A Course in Miracles* and to Jesus himself. However the good news, reflective of the original Good News of the Atonement, is that our attempts to keep his love away all come to nought. In the end, the "attraction of love for love" (T-12.VIII) proves stronger than the attraction of guilt for fear. "Bright Stranger" therefore speaks to and for all of us, as it reminds us that our resistance to Jesus' love will fall before "His soft appeal," and we will remember his love and find our Self:

Bright Stranger

Strange was my Love to me. For when He came
I did not know Him. And He seemed to me
To be but an intruder on my peace.
I did not see the gifts He brought, nor hear
His soft appeal. I tried to shut Him out
With locks and keys that merely fell away
Before his coming. I could not escape
The gentleness with which He looked at me.
I asked Him in unwillingly, and turned
Away from Him. But he held out His hand
And asked me to remember Him. In me
An ancient Name began to stir and break
Across my mind in gold. The light embraced
Me deep in silence till He spoke the Word,
And then at last I recognized my Lord.

(*The Gifts of God*, p. 43)

APPENDIX

RESISTANCE:
HOW ONE STUDIES *A COURSE IN MIRACLES* WITHOUT REALLY LEARNING IT[1]

Gloria and Kenneth Wapnick, Ph.D.

Although the term *resistance* appears infrequently in *A Course in Miracles*, it is nonetheless a key concept in the process of students' learning the mind-changing lessons of forgiveness that are the Course's central teaching. Indeed, it is the only concept that can satisfactorily explain a phenomenon experienced by most (if not all) students of the Course at some point or another in their work with it. This is the seeming paradox, on the one hand, of consciously and most sincerely attempting to learn, live, and practice the Course principles under the guidance of Jesus or the Holy Spirit, while on the other hand, experiencing the ongoing frustration of *not* doing just that. Most spiritual seekers are familiar with the famous words of St. Paul, who exclaimed out of this same sense of frustration: "For the good that I would I do not: but the evil which I would not, that I do" (Romans 7:19). This article explores the issue of resistance in Course students' efforts to put into practice its principles of

1. Reprinted, with minor modifications, from *The Lighthouse*, June 1999.

forgiveness as taught by their Inner Teacher, the Holy Spirit.

As with so many other areas that touch on the *process* of healing in *A Course in Miracles*, the work of Sigmund Freud offers us many parallels that underscore the importance of understanding the dynamics of the problem and its solution. Very early in his psychoanalytic work, Freud observed that his patients were not improving, despite the insights he was offering them as to the cause of their neuroses. It eventually dawned on him that the problem lay in the fact that the patients did not *want* to get better, a dynamic he termed *resistance*:

> ...the [therapeutic] situation led me at once to the theory that *by means of my psychical* [i.e., psychological] *work I had to overcome a psychical force in the patients which was opposed to the pathogenic ideas becoming conscious.* ...This work of overcoming resistances is the essential function of analytic treatment...(*Studies on Hysteria* (with J. Breuer), 1893, Vol. II, p. 268; *Introductory Lectures on Psychoanalysis*, 1917, Vol. XVI, p. 451).[2]

---

2. All references to Freud are taken from *The Standard Edition of the Complete Psychological Works of Sigmund Freud* (London: Hogarth Press, 1953).

Indeed, in several places in *A Course in Miracles* Jesus lets us know that *he* knows that we will experience resistance to his teachings. We present a few of these, beginning with this statement from the "Rules for Decision" in Chapter 30 of the text:

> And if you find resistance strong and dedication weak, you are not ready. *Do not fight yourself* (T-30.I.1:6-7).

Repeatedly throughout the workbook for students, Jesus alerts us to our potential resistance to the radical ideas he is teaching. In fact, in the Introduction itself he states:

> Some of the ideas the workbook presents you will find hard to believe, and others may seem to be quite startling. This does not matter. ...Remember only this; you need not believe the ideas, you need not accept them, and you need not even welcome them. Some of them you may actively resist (W-pI.in.8:1-2; 9:1-2).

One other example from the workbook:

> Your mind is no longer wholly untrained. You are quite ready to learn the form of exercise we will use today, but you may find that you will encounter strong resistance. The reason is very simple. While you practice in this way, you leave behind everything that you now believe, and all the thoughts that you have made up. Properly

> speaking, this is the release from hell. Yet perceived through the ego's eyes, it is loss of identity and a descent into hell (W-pI.44.5).

In the manual for teachers we find a similar statement from Jesus, alerting his students to the fear involved in accepting his teachings; in this case it is the principle that the cause of sickness is found in the mind and not the body:

> The resistance to recognizing this is enormous, because the existence of the world as you perceive it depends on the body being the decision maker (M-5.II.1:7).

The resistance referred to in the above passages is directly related to the fear of losing our personal specialness and individual uniqueness, the letting go of which is the final step before one can awaken from the dream of separation.

Resistance—the unconscious attempt to sabotage what alone will help—is so surprising as to be almost unbelievable, as Freud himself observed in this clever, quasi-Platonic dialogue with himself, taken from *The Question of Lay Analysis*, written in 1926:

> It will then be your fate to make a discovery for which you were not prepared.
>
> "And what may that be?"
>
> That you have been deceived in your patient; that you cannot count in the slightest on his

> collaboration and compliance; that he is ready to place every possible difficulty in the way of your common work—in a word, that he has no wish whatever to be cured.
>
> "Well! that is the craziest thing you have told me yet. And I do not believe it either. The patient who is suffering so much, who complains so movingly about his troubles, who is making so great a sacrifice for the treatment—you say he has no wish to be cured! But of course you do not mean what you say."
>
> Calm yourself! I *do* mean it. What I said was the truth—not the whole truth, no doubt, but a very noteworthy part of it. The patient wants to be cured—but he also wants not to be.... They [the patients] complain of their illness but exploit it with all their strength; and if someone tries to take it away from them they defend it like the proverbial lioness with her young (*The Question of Lay Analysis,* 1926, Vol. XX, pp. 221-22).

This phenomenon, which is so clear to the psychoanalyst or psychotherapist, is not always recognized in discussions of the spiritual life. And yet how could it *not* be just as present in spiritual seekers as in psychotherapeutic patients, since undoing the thought system of guilt, anxiety, and fear is common to both disciplines? And how could the undoing of this resistance *not* be among the most significant aspects to anyone's spiritual path, since the ego with which we all identify *is* the impediment to our progress? In the pamphlet *Psychotherapy: Purpose, Process and Practice*, Jesus comments on the parallel goals of religion and psychotherapy:

> Religion is experience; psychotherapy is experience. At the highest levels they become one. Neither is truth itself, but both can lead to truth. What can be necessary to find truth, which remains perfectly obvious, but to remove the seeming obstacles to true awareness? (P-2.II.2:4-7)

These "seeming obstacles" are our *resistance*, described in the pamphlet, in the context of preserving one's self-concept in the face of the threat of real therapeutic change (P-2.in.3:3; P-2.I.2:4-9).

Thus we see that an important component of our resistance to learning the teachings of *A Course in Miracles* is our need to suffer and be guilty, what in the *Psychotherapy* pamphlet Jesus refers to as "the hanging-on to guilt, its hugging-close and sheltering, its loving protection and alert defense" (P-2.VI.1:3), or in Freud's words below, the "powerful need for punishment":

> ...the impression derived from the work of analysis [is] that the patient who puts up a resistance is so often unaware of that resistance. Not only the fact of the resistance is unconscious to him, however, but its motives as well. We were obliged to

> search out these motives or motive, and to our surprise we found them in a powerful need for punishment.... The practical significance of this discovery is not less than its theoretical one, for the need for punishment is the worst enemy of our therapeutic efforts. It is satisfied by the suffering which is linked to the neurosis, and for that reason holds fast to being ill.... [It is the] "need to be ill or to suffer"... The patient must not become well but must remain ill (*New Introductory Lectures on Psychoanalysis*, 1933, Vol. XXII, p. 108; *An Outline of Psychoanalysis*, 1940, Vol. XXIII, pp. 178-80).

This attraction to guilt in ourselves is central to *A Course in Miracles*' teachings on the ego thought system, for guilt witnesses to the seeming reality of the separation. The experience of punishment—real or imagined—justifies our belief in guilt and therefore reinforces the fundamental premise of the ego's existence. To let it go would be tantamount ultimately to letting go of the belief in the reality of a personal self, and thus we *resist* doing so, not to mention *resist* the one (or One) helping us to do just that. Jesus comments on this phenomenon, referring to his own life:

> Many thought I was attacking them, even though it was apparent I was not. An insane learner learns strange lessons. What you must recognize

> is that when you do not share a thought system, you are weakening it. Those who believe in it therefore perceive this as an attack on them. This is because everyone identifies himself with his thought system, and every thought system centers on what you believe you are (T-6.V-B.1:5-9).

Needless to say, when we believe we are being attacked, we feel justified in attacking back, and almost always *do*, literally in *self*-defense.

And so we are led to another significant effect of a student's resistance to *A Course in Miracles*: the need to prove the Course wrong. Underlying this dynamic is the hope that if it is wrong then we do not have to do what it says and change from our ego's way of thinking. Freud, too, in his monumental *The Interpretation of Dreams* remarked on this interesting phenomenon in his patients: the need to prove the analyst wrong:

> One of the two motive forces leading to such dreams is the wish that I may be wrong. These dreams appear regularly in the course of my treatments when a patient is in a state of resistance to me; and I can count almost certainly on provoking one of them after I have explained to a patient for the first time my theory that dreams are fulfillments of wishes. Indeed, it is to be expected that the same thing will happen to some of the readers of the present book: they will be quite ready to have one of their wishes frustrated

> in a dream if only their wish that I may be wrong can be fulfilled (*The Interpretation of Dreams,* 1900, Vol. IV, pp. 157-58).

This form of resistance as it is expressed in students of *A Course in Miracles*, can take the form of arguing with the material, especially focusing on the *form* as a means of ignoring the *content*. Readers of Kenneth's *Absence from Felicity: The Story of Helen Schucman and Her Scribing of A Course in Miracles* may recall the story he tells there (pp. 255-57) of Helen's attempts to do just that during the early weeks of the dictation. Space considerations prevent its full retelling here, but suffice it to say that Helen used a seeming grammatical error on Jesus' part as a justification for her rejecting the material. She wrote:

> This real grammatical error makes me suspicious of the genuineness of these notes.

Jesus' response, greatly abbreviated here was:

> The reason it came out that way, is because you are projecting ... your own anger, which has nothing to do with these notes. *You* made the error, because you are not feeling loving, so you want me to sound silly, so you won't have to pay attention.

Therefore, when students of *A Course in Miracles* are *not* experiencing the positive effects "promised" by Jesus in his Course, it is not because *A Course in Miracles* has failed them. Rather it is because of their unconscious resistance to what it is truly saying. When Helen complained to Jesus that she was not being helped by his teachings, he responded in the following words, presented here in the edited form of the published Course:

> You may complain that this course is not sufficiently specific for you to understand and use. Yet perhaps you have not done what it specifically advocates. This is a not a course in the play of ideas, but in their practical application (T-11.VIII.5:1-3).

As Cassius said to his co-conspirator:

> The fault, dear Brutus, is not in our stars,
> But in ourselves. . . . (*Julius Caesar*, I,ii).

Or as Jesus so emphatically states near the end of Chapter 27 of the text:

> The secret of salvation is but this: That you are doing this unto yourself (T-27.VIII.10:1).

It was clear to Freud, just as Jesus makes it clear in *A Course in Miracles*, that a mere intellectual understanding of one's problem is not enough. Rather, it is essential that the resistance to letting go of the problem be uncovered and looked at:

It is true that in the earliest days of analytic technique we took an intellectualist view of the situation.... It was a severe disappointment when the expected success was not forthcoming.... Indeed, telling and describing his [the patient's] repressed trauma to him did not even result in any recollection of it coming into his mind.... After this, there was no choice but to cease attributing to the fact of knowing, in itself, the importance that had previously been given to it and to place the emphasis on the resistances which had in the past brought about the state of not knowing and which were still ready to defend that state. *Conscious knowledge ... was powerless against those resistances...* (Freud, *On Beginning the Treatment*, 1913, Vol. XII, pp. 141-42).

How do we remove the resistance?... by discovering it and showing it to the patient.... If I say to you: "Look up at the sky! There's a balloon there!" you will discover it much more easily than if I simply tell you to look up and see if you can see anything. In the same way, a student who is looking through a microscope for the first time is instructed by his teacher as to what he will see; otherwise he does not see it at all, though it is there and visible (Freud, *Introductory Lectures on Psychoanalysis*, 1917, Vol. XVI, p. 437; italics mine).

This is the heart of Jesus' teaching message in *A Course in Miracles:* uncovering the ego so that we may see our identification with it. Indeed, this process of looking at the ego *is* the essence of forgiveness:

> Forgiveness...is still, and quietly does nothing. ... It merely looks, and waits, and judges not (W-pII.1.4:1,3).

In this all-important passage from the text, Jesus illustrates the importance of "discovering and showing" the ego to his students as the prerequisite for healing:

> No one can escape from illusions unless he looks at them, for not looking is the way they are protected.... We are ready to look more closely at the ego's thought system because together we have the lamp that will dispel it, and since you realize you do not want it, you must be ready.... The "dynamics" of the ego will be our lesson for a while, for we must look first at this to see beyond it, since you have made it real. We will undo this error quietly together, and then look beyond it to truth.
>
> What is healing but the removal of all that stands in the way of knowledge? And how else can one dispel illusions except by looking at them directly, without protecting them? (T-11.V.1:1,3,5–2:2)

Again, looking at the ego means looking at the resistance, realizing how much we have *wanted* our ego and not God, and what this desire for specialness has cost us. Only then will we be able to truly move beyond our resistance and find the peace of God.

Finally, it should be clear that the process of undoing this resistance is one that occurs over time, and requires the gentle patience that is one of the principal characteristics not only of Jesus or the Holy Spirit, but also of the advanced teacher of God (M-4.I-A,IV,VIII). Freud clearly recognized this in his analytic work:

> In the first place, we must reflect that a psychical [i.e., psychological] resistance, especially one that has been in force for a long time, can only be resolved slowly and by degrees, and we must wait patiently....One must allow the patient time to become more conversant with this resistance with which he has now become acquainted, to *work through* it...(*Studies on Hysteria* (with J. Breuer), 1893, Vol. II, p. 282; *Remembering, Repeating and Working-Through*, 1914, Vol. XII, p. 155).

And in several places Jesus lets his students know that, in the world of time, the process of accepting the Atonement through forgiveness *must* occur over time, because of the imagined fear of living without the ego.

The closing paragraphs of Chapter 1 of the text, originally meant for Helen Schucman's and William Thetford's *study* of the material, make it quite clear how Jesus sees the process of study and practice of the Course in light of our fearing what he is truly teaching us about leaving our egos aside (the *means)* and returning to God (the *end*):

> This is a course in mind training. All learning involves attention and study at some level. Some of the later parts of the course rest too heavily on these earlier sections not to require their careful study. You will also need them for preparation. Without this, you may become much too fearful of what is to come to make constructive use of it....
>
> A solid foundation is necessary because of the confusion between fear and awe to which I have already referred, and which is often made. ... Some of the later steps in this course ... involve a more direct approach to God Himself. It would be unwise to start on these steps without careful preparation, or awe will be confused with fear, and the experience will be more traumatic than beatific. Healing is of God in the end. The means are being carefully explained to you. Revelation may occasionally reveal the end to you, but to reach it the means are needed (T-1.VII.4:1-5; 5:1,7-11).

In discussing the six stages in the development of trust—a summary of the Atonement path—Jesus emphasizes the great difficulty in a student's reaching the final stage (the attainment of the real world):

> He thought he learned willingness, but now he sees that he does not know what the willingness is for. And now he must attain a state that *may remain impossible to reach for a long, long time.* He must learn to lay all judgment aside, and ask only what he really wants in every circumstance (M-4.I-A.7:6-8; italics mine).

In conclusion, therefore, just as it was clear to Freud a century ago, and to analysts and therapists ever since, it should be clear to all spiritual seekers that the best intentions in the world are not sufficient to bring about the spiritual goal of our awakening from the darkness (T-18.IV.2:1-2). Rather, what is required is the willingness to examine—*gently* and *patiently*—every aspect of our ego thought system that seeks to conceal the light (T-24.in.2:1-2), most especially our *resistance* to this very light. In introducing workbook Lesson 185—"I want the peace of God"—Jesus says:

> To say these words is nothing. But to mean these words is everything (W-pI.185.1:1-2).

A Course in Miracles, happily for us, helps us to discover and reinforce that part of our minds (*the right mind*) that truly does mean these words, at the same time we are being taught that the other part (*the wrong mind*) will never bring us the happiness and peace we most truly desire. Thus, by heeding Jesus' appeal to our choosing the right mind over the wrong mind, the Holy Spirit over the ego, the resistance to losing our illusory self is finally undone. And we are free! And we are free at last!

THE DIVER[1]

Gloria and Kenneth Wapnick, Ph.D.

In our previous article in the June edition of "The Lighthouse," we discussed the resistance that students of *A Course in Miracles* inevitably have towards not only understanding what Jesus is teaching, but also in applying his principles of forgiveness to their everyday lives. In the current article we explore in more depth one aspect of this resistance: the fear—in one sense, at least, a justified fear—of looking at the ego's thought system of guilt and hate.

Friedrich Schiller, the great German poet, dramatist, and man of letters, wrote a ballad in 1797 called "Der Taucher" ("The Diver"), which outside Germany is probably more well known in the musical setting of Franz Schubert. It is the tragic tale of a young squire who accepts a royal challenge and successfully dives to the bottom of a raging sea to retrieve a golden goblet thrown there by the king. He tempts fate a second time when the cruel king says he can have the hand of his beautiful daughter if he but repeats his previous success. Sadly this time, the young man does

---

1. Reprinted, with minor modifications, from *The Lighthouse*, September 1999.

not return from the depths. Before his fatal dive from the cliff, however, he prophetically says the following to the king, speaking of the raging torrent from which he has just escaped:

> For below it is dreadful
> And man should not tempt the gods;
> And should never desire to behold
> What they mercifully cover with night and horror.[2]

Schiller's work was an ongoing source of inspiration to German intellectuals, although he is most remembered today in the non-German-speaking world only for his poem, "Ode to Joy," immortalized by Beethoven in his Ninth Symphony. Among those inspired by Schiller were Sigmund Freud and C. G. Jung, the latter specifically remarking on the above four lines as reflecting "the real meaning of that glimpse into the abysses of human nature."[3] One can easily read deeper meaning into Schiller's verse, and see depicted there the frightening depths of the human psyche—*it is dreadful*—and then the almost equally

---

2. Schiller's original German: *Aber da unten ist's fuerchterlich,/ und der Mensch versuche die Goetter nicht,/und begehe nimmer und nimmer zu schauen,/was sie gnaedig bedecken mit Nacht und Grauen.*
3. *Psychological Types*, Volume VI of *The Collected Works* (Princeton University Press, Princeton, NJ, 1971), p. 96.

frightening defense—*night and horror*—that enables one to survive, albeit barely, in the world.

Though Freud was the first psychologist to expose fully the horrors of the unconscious ego mind, he was certainly not the first to have made such observations. Among many, many others, we may cite the German 18th-century romantic poet Novalis, who said: "One is necessarily terrified when one casts a glance into the depths of the mind."[4] Indeed, Freud was properly terrified at what he saw in his self-analysis, as well as in his patients, and described the unconscious with adjectives like *horrible, perverse, primitive, savage, evil, disgusting, monstrous, dangerous,* and *frightening*, and with phrases such as *a cauldron full of seething excitations*, filled with *chaos, half-tamed demons, strange and uncanny things,* and *evil spirits*.

In *A Course in Miracles*, we also find Jesus frequently offering us a glimpse into the nature of the abyss that is the terrifying thought system of the ego mind. It is not a pretty picture. Guilt is ugly and uglier still, reflecting the monstrously sinful deed it claims to truly express—nothing less than the murder of God and the crucifixion of His Son. Here are two examples that express the horror of the ego's vicious and

---

4. Quoted in L.L. Whyte, *The Unconscious before Freud* (Basic Books, New York, 1960), p. 121.

murderous world of guilt. Let the reader beware; this is strong stuff:

> Fear's messengers are trained through terror, and they tremble when their master calls on them to serve him. For fear is merciless even to its friends. Its messengers steal guiltily away in hungry search of guilt, for they are kept cold and starving and made very vicious by their master, who allows them to feast only upon what they return to him. No little shred of guilt escapes their hungry eyes. And in their savage search for sin they pounce on any living thing they see, and carry it screaming to their master, to be devoured.... they will bring you word of bones and skin and flesh. They have been taught to seek for the corruptible, and to return with gorges filled with things decayed and rotted. To them such things are beautiful, because they seem to allay their savage pangs of hunger. For they are frantic with the pain of fear, and would avert the punishment of him who sends them forth by offering him what they hold dear (T-19.IV-A.12:3-7; 13:2-5).
>
> Hate is specific. There must be a thing to be attacked. An enemy must be perceived in such a form he can be touched and seen and heard, and ultimately killed. When hatred rests upon a thing, it calls for death....Fear is insatiable, consuming everything its eyes behold, seeing itself in

> everything, compelled to turn upon itself and to destroy.
>
> Who sees a brother as a body sees him as fear's symbol. And he will attack, because what he beholds is his own fear external to himself, poised to attack, and howling to unite with him again. Mistake not the intensity of rage projected fear must spawn. It shrieks in wrath, and claws the air in frantic hope it can reach to its maker and devour him (W-pI.161.7:1–8:4).

This inner world of horror is so intolerable that it demands a defense to protect us. And so the ego promises us protection from this *dreadful below* if we but follow its deceitful counsel and escape to its made-up world, the physical universe: the horrific home of bodies, special relationships, and death. And yet this world appears to be outside our guilty minds, and thus identifying with it brings the appearance of relief and safety from our perceived sin. In a number of places the Course refers to these—the ego's problem and its answer—as two dreams: the world's dream (the body) covering the ego's secret dream (the mind) (e.g., T-27.VII.11:4–12:6). Borrowing Schiller's imagery again, we may say that the outer world of horror covers the dreaded inner sea of horror. Thus are we offered a double shield against what the ego would never have us *really* look at. For beyond its twin worlds of horror and horror lies the ego's secret fear:

that we might come to recognize the Love of God that is our true reality and our true Home, reflected in our split minds by the Holy Spirit. Yet one cannot awaken to that Love without first going through the two worlds of dreams, as we see in this passage from the prose poem, *The Gifts of God*, which clearly expresses the fear of looking at the first dream:

> They [the world's dreams] content the frightened dreamer for a little while, and let him not remember the first dream [the mind's dream of sin, guilt, and fear—Schiller's *below it is dreadful*] which gifts of fear but offer him again. The seeming solace of illusions' gifts are now his armor [Schiller's *cover* (of) *night and horror*], and the sword he holds to save himself from waking. For before he could awaken, he would first be forced to call to mind the first dream once again (*The Gifts of God*, p. 120).

Because of this fear—totally made up, although unbeknownst to us—we retreat into the physical world of pseudo-problems and pseudo-answers, of seeming-life and seeming-death, and remain still further from the truth that is buried in our minds beneath the two dreams. Thus, this underlying torrent that constitutes the secret dream is not recognized, as we choose *not* to dive. It is an immutable psychological law, however, that what remains unexposed in the unconscious, festers within, only to rear its ugly head in our daily lives. Our judgments against ourselves, our "secret sins and hidden hates" (T-31.VIII.9:2), become projected out in the form of judgment, condemnation, and the need to criticize and find fault—all these are simply the inevitable result of such "protection" of our own unforgiveness:

> The [unforgiving] thought protects projection, tightening its chains, so that distortions are more veiled and more obscure; less easily accessible to doubt, and further kept from reason (W-pII.1.2:3).

As Jung observed, in discussing the tragic implications of denying the unconscious (or the "shadow"):

> The "man without a shadow" is statistically the commonest human type, one who imagines he actually is only what he cares to know about himself. Unfortunately neither the so-called religious man nor the man of scientific pretensions forms an exception to this rule.[5]

In the words of *The Song of Prayer*, companion to *A Course in Miracles*, Jung's description reflects the hateful dynamic of forgiveness-to-destroy, wherein people consciously believe they are being loving, forgiving, and peaceful, when all they are truly doing is projecting their unconscious hatred onto the world.

---

5. *On the Nature of the Psyche*, Volume VIII of *The Collected Works* (Princeton University Press, Princeton, NJ, 1969), p. 208.

Unfortunately, the history of world religions and nation states—past and present—flows with blood in the name of such seeming qualities as love, forgiveness, and peace. It would be difficult to underestimate the tragic consequences (T-3.I.2:3) of such denial, and the world bears painful witness to its efficacy. It is therefore essential that this dynamic be understood so that the mistake can be finally undone. Not doing the *inner* work of forgiveness, of asking the Holy Spirit's help to accept His correction in our *minds* for our *mis*-thoughts, of learning to accept the Atonement for ourselves, is the invitation for the ego to conceal its pseudo-reality of sin, guilt, fear, and hatred behind the mantle of respectability—equally illusory—of spirituality and religion. And all the time we are so sure our position is right and just, we are concealing the seething cauldron of hatred that lies in the sea just below the threshold of our awareness.

Thus we may read *A Course in Miracles* as Jesus asking us to be divers, meaning that he asks us to take his hand as we dive—albeit gently and carefully—into the abyss of the ego thought system. With his love by our side, we expose the mind's seemingly raging torrent of sin, guilt, fear, and murder that *mercifully* lies just beyond the cover of the world's *night and horror*—the ostensible pain of living in this bodily world of specialness and hate. And so it is that the only way one could truly respond to the Holy Spirit's guidance is by retracing with Him the mad course into insanity, walking *up* the ladder that the separation led us *down* (T-18.I.8:3-5; T-28.III.1:2), after *first* recognizing we *are* down, and what being down really means. The process of forgiveness, therefore, calls on us to examine—without judgment—the shadowy world of our special relationships that is the mirror of the inner world of guilt's dark shadow. This is the guilt-driven world we would then see:

> The acceptance of guilt into the mind of God's Son was the beginning of the separation, as the acceptance of the Atonement is its end. The world you see is the delusional system of those made mad by guilt. Look carefully at this world, and you will realize that this is so. For this world is the symbol of punishment, and all the laws that seem to govern it are the laws of death. Children are born into it through pain and in pain. Their growth is attended by suffering, and they learn of sorrow and separation and death. Their minds seem to be trapped in their brain, and its powers to decline if their bodies are hurt. They seem to love, yet they desert and are deserted. They appear to lose what they love, perhaps the most insane belief of all. And their bodies wither and gasp and are laid in the ground, and are no more. Not one of them but has thought that God is cruel (T-13.in.2).

And so in taking the Holy Spirit's hand, as it were, we are led into the depths of the ego's thought system —the defense *against* the Holy Spirit's correction— but the ego (the symbol of our fear) fights back in order to preserve its identity. *A Course in Miracles* teaches us that we need to look at the darkness that we believe is within our minds, but the ego says to us in response that if we do so, we shall, like Medusa's victims, turn to stone and be destroyed. This aspect of the ego's defensive arsenal must be seen for the trick it is, otherwise we shall be forever afraid of this next step, leading inevitably to our choosing the ego's forgiveness-to-destroy—wherein, again, we attack but call it love, forgiveness, and peace—instead of the true forgiveness offered us by the Holy Spirit. These are but a few expressions of the ego's tactic of inducing fear:

> As you approach the Beginning, you feel the fear of the destruction of your thought system upon you as if it were the fear of death (T-3.VII.5:10).

> The ego is, therefore, particularly likely to attack you when you react lovingly, because it has evaluated you as unloving and you are going against its judgment. The ego will attack your motives as soon as they become clearly out of accord with its perception of you. This is when it will shift abruptly from suspiciousness to viciousness, since its uncertainty is increased (T-9.VII.4:5-7).

> As the light comes nearer you will rush to darkness, shrinking from the truth, sometimes retreating to the lesser forms of fear, and sometimes to stark terror (T-18.III.2:1).

> Loudly the ego tells you not to look inward, for if you do your eyes will light on sin, and God will strike you blind. This you believe, and so you do not look....Loudly indeed the ego claims it is; too loudly and too often (T-21.IV.2:3-4,6).

Yet a dream cannot escape its source, which is always the mind of the dreamer: where the dream begins and the only place it can truly be undone (T-27.VII.12:6). Looking within with Jesus we realize, thankfully, that this fear is all made up: the ego is *not* this swirling mass of chaotic and demonic energy, but like the wicked witch in *The Wizard of Oz*, simply an insignificant and harmless mass of nothing that dissolves in the gentle presence of truth. It is the simple change of mind—turning *from* the ego and *to* the Holy Spirit—that removes the "reality" from the ego's thought system. Thus, Jesus urges us to look at the seeming content of the secret dream (T-17.IV.9:1), and comforts us not to be afraid of what only *appears* to be within:

> Be not afraid, therefore, for what you will be looking at is the source of fear, and you are beginning to learn that fear is not real (T-11.V.2:3).

> Do not be afraid to look within. The ego tells you all is black with guilt within you, and bids you not to look. Instead, it bids you look upon your brothers, and see the guilt in them. Yet this you cannot do without remaining blind. For those who see their brothers in the dark, and guilty in the dark in which they shroud them, are too afraid to look upon the light within. Within you is not what you believe is there, and what you put your faith in. Within you is the holy sign of perfect faith your Father has in you.... Can you see guilt where God knows there is perfect innocence? You can deny His knowledge, but you cannot change it. Look, then, upon the light He placed within you, and learn that what you feared was there has been replaced with love (T-13.IX.8:1-7,11-13).

When at last we dive down into our minds by shifting the perception of our relationships, Jesus' love being our guide and our safety, we realize gratefully that there was indeed nothing there—nothing to fear, nothing to defend against. Only then do we understand that the precious goblet and beautiful princess are *already* our treasure—sought for within the mind, not in the world; to be accepted, not won. And we give thanks "that for all this [we] gave up *nothing*!" (T-16.VI.11:4).

INDEX OF REFERENCES TO *A COURSE IN MIRACLES*

text

text (continued)

text (continued)

workbook for students

manual for teachers

clarification of terms

Psychotherapy: Purpose, Process and Practice

The Gifts of God

Foundation for A Course in Miracles®

Kenneth Wapnick *received his Ph.D. in Clinical Psychology in 1968 from Adelphi University. He was a close friend and associate of Helen Schucman and William Thetford, the two people whose joining together was the immediate stimulus for the scribing of A Course in Miracles. Kenneth has been involved with A Course in Miracles since 1973, writing, teaching, and integrating its principles with his practice of psychotherapy. He is on the Executive Board of the Foundation for Inner Peace, publishers of A Course in Miracles.*

In 1983, with his wife Gloria, he began the Foundation for A Course in Miracles, and in 1984 this evolved into a Teaching and Healing Center in Crompond, New York, which was quickly outgrown. In 1988 they opened the Academy and Retreat Center in upstate New York. In 1995 they began the Institute for Teaching Inner Peace through A Course in Miracles, an educational corporation chartered by the New York State Board of Regents. In 2001 the Foundation moved to Temecula, California and shifted its emphasis to electronic teaching. The Foundation is the copyright holder of A Course in Miracles, and also publishes a quarterly newsletter, "The Lighthouse," which is available free of charge. The following is Kenneth's and Gloria's vision of the Foundation.

In our early years of studying *A Course in Miracles,* as well as teaching and applying its principles in our respective professions of psychotherapy, and teaching and school administration, it seemed evident that this was not the simplest of thought systems to understand. This was so not only in the intellectual grasp of its teachings, but perhaps more importantly in the application of these teachings to our personal lives. Thus, it appeared to us from the beginning that the Course lent itself to teaching, parallel to the ongoing teachings of the Holy Spirit in the daily opportunities within our relationships, which are discussed in the early pages of the manual for teachers.

One day several years ago while Helen Schucman and I (Kenneth) were discussing these ideas, she shared a vision that she had had of a teaching center as a white temple with a gold cross atop it. Although it was clear that this image was symbolic, we understood it to be representative of what the teaching center was to be: a place where the person of Jesus and his message in *A Course in Miracles* would be manifest. We have sometimes seen an image of a lighthouse shining its light into the sea, calling to it those passers-by who sought it. For us, this light is the Course's teaching of forgiveness, which we would hope to share with those who are drawn to the Foundation's form of teaching and its vision of *A Course in Miracles.*

This vision entails the belief that Jesus gave the Course at this particular time in this particular form for several reasons. These include:

1) the necessity of healing the mind of its belief that attack is salvation; this is accomplished through forgiveness, the undoing of our belief in the reality of separation and guilt.

2) emphasizing the importance of Jesus and/or the Holy Spirit as our loving and gentle Teacher, and developing a personal relationship with this Teacher.

3) correcting the errors of Christianity, particularly where it has emphasized suffering, sacrifice, separation, and sacrament as being inherent in God's plan for salvation.

Our thinking has always been inspired by Plato (and his mentor Socrates), both the man and his teachings. Plato's Academy was a place where serious and thoughtful people came to study his philosophy in an atmosphere conducive to their learning, and then returned to their professions to implement what they were taught by the great philosopher. Thus, by integrating abstract philosophical ideals with experience, Plato's school seemed to be the perfect model for the teaching center that we directed for so many years.

We therefore see the Foundation's principal purpose as being to help students of *A Course in Miracles* deepen their understanding of its thought system, conceptually and experientially, so that they may be more effective instruments of Jesus' teaching in their own lives. Since teaching forgiveness without experiencing it is empty, one of the Foundation's specific goals is to help facilitate the process whereby people may be better able to know that their own sins are forgiven and that they are truly loved by God. Thus is the Holy Spirit able to extend His Love through them to others.

Responding in part to the "electronic revolution," we have taken the Foundation's next step in our move to Temecula, California. With this move to a non-residential setting we are shifting our focus, though not exclusively, from totally live presentations to electronic and digital forms of teaching in order to maximize the benefits of the burgeoning field of electronic media communication. This will allow us to increase our teaching outreach, the *content* of which will remain the same, allowing its *form* to adapt to the 21st century.

RELATED MATERIAL ON *A COURSE IN MIRACLES®*

By Kenneth Wapnick, Ph.D.

Books

(For full descriptions please see our Web site at www.facim.org or call or write for our free catalog)

CHRISTIAN PSYCHOLOGY IN *A COURSE IN MIRACLES.®* Second edition, enlarged.
ISBN 0-933291-14-0 • #B-1• Paperback • 90 pages $5
Audio version of the second edition of the book,
read by Kenneth Wapnick • #T2 $10

Available also in Spanish:
PSICOLOGIA CRISTIANA EN *UN CURSO EN MILAGROS*
ISBN 0-933291-17-5 • #B-1s • Paperback • 114 pages $5

A TALK GIVEN ON *A COURSE IN MIRACLES*:® An Introduction. Seventh edition.
ISBN 0-933291-16-7 • #B-3 • Paperback • 131 pages $6

Available also in Spanish:
UNA INTRODUCCION BASICA A *UN CURSO EN MILAGROS*
ISBN 0-933291-10-8 • #B-3s • Paperback • 159 pages $6

Available also in Portuguese:
UMA INTRODUÇÃO BÁSICA A *UM CURSO EM MILAGRES*
ISBN 0-933291-27-2 • #B-3p • Paperback • 145 pages $5

Available also in German:*
EINFÜHRUNG IN *EIN KURS IN WUNDERN®*

Available also in Dutch:
INLEIDING TOT *A COURSE IN MIRACLES®*
Order from: Ankh-Hermes bv • Postbus 125 • 7400 AC Deventer • Netherlands

---

* ***All German translations may be ordered from***:
Greuthof Verlag und Vertrieb GmbH • Herrenweg 2 • D 79261 Gutach i. Br. • Germany • Tel. 07681-6025 • FAX 07681-6027.

Available also in French:
INTRODUCTION GENERALE A *UN COURS SUR LES MIRACLES*
ISBN 0-933291-26-4 • #B-3f • Paperback • 145 pages $6

Available also in Danish:
INTRODUKTION TIL *ET KURSES I MIRAKLER®*
Order from: SphinX Publishers • Løvstræde 8 • 1152 København K • Denmark

Available also in Italian:
INTRODUZIONE A *UN CORSO IN MIRACOLI®*
Order from: Gruppo Editoriale Armenia • Via Valtellina, 63 • 20129 Milano, Ilaly

GLOSSARY-INDEX FOR *A COURSE IN MIRACLES®* Fifth edition, revised and enlarged.
ISBN 0-933291-03-5 • #B-4 • Softcover • 349 pages $10

Available also in Spanish:
GLOSARIO-INDICE PARA *UN CURSO EN MILAGROS*
ISBN 0-933291-20-5 • #B-4s • Paperback • 245 pages $10

Available also in German:
GLOSSAR ZU *EIN KURS IN WUNDERN®*

FORGIVENESS AND JESUS: The Meeting Place of *A Course in Miracles®* and Christianity. Sixth edition.
ISBN 0-933291-13-2 • #B-5 • Paperback • 399 pages $16

Available also in Spanish:
EL PERDON Y JESUS: El punto de encuentro entre *Un curso en milagros* y el cristianismo
ISBN 0-933291-23-X • #B-5s • Paperback • 435 pages $16

Available also in German:
DIE VERGEBUNG UND JESUS

THE FIFTY MIRACLE PRINCIPLES OF *A COURSE IN MIRACLES®* Fifth edition.
ISBN 0-933291-15-9 • #B-6 • Paperback • 107 pages $8

Available also in Spanish:
LOS CINCUENTA PRINCIPIOS DEL MILAGRO DE *UN CURSO EN MILAGROS*
ISBN 0-933291-19-1 • #B-6s • Paperback • 139 pages $8

Available also in German:
WUNDER ALS WEG

AWAKEN FROM THE DREAM. Second Edition. Gloria and Kenneth Wapnick.
ISBN 0-933291-04-3 • #B-7 • Paperback • 132 pages $10

Available in German:
VON TRAUM ERWACHEN

THE OBSTACLES TO PEACE.
ISBN 0-933291-05-1 • #B-8 • Paperback • 295 pages $12

LOVE DOES NOT CONDEMN: The World, the Flesh, and the Devil According to Platonism, Christianity, Gnosticism, and *A Course in Miracles*.®
ISBN 0-933291-07-8 • #B-9 • Hardcover • 614 pages $25

A VAST ILLUSION: Time According to *A Course in Miracles*.® Second edition.
ISBN 0-933291-09-4 • #B-10 • Paperback • 345 pages $12

Available also in German:
DIE ILLUSION DER ZEIT

ABSENCE FROM FELICITY: The Story of Helen Schucman and Her Scribing of *A Course in Miracles*.® Second Edition.
ISBN 0-933291-08-6 • #B-11 • Paperback • 498 pages $17

Available also in German:
JENSEITS DER GLÜCKSELIGKEIT

OVEREATING: A Dialogue. An Application of the Principles of *A Course in Miracles*.® Second Edition.
ISBN 0-933291-11-6 • #B-12 • Paperback • 70 pages $5

A COURSE IN MIRACLES® AND CHRISTIANITY: A DIALOGUE. Kenneth Wapnick and W. Norris Clarke, S.J.
ISBN 0-933291-18-3 • #B-13 • Paperback • 110 pages $7

Available also in Spanish:
UN CURSO DE MILAGROS Y EL CRISTIANISMO: Un Dialogo
ISBN 0-933291-22-1 • #B-13s • Paperback • 117 pages $7

Available also in German:
EIN KURS IN WUNDERN UND DAS CHRISTENTUM - EIN DIALOG

THE MOST COMMONLY ASKED QUESTIONS ABOUT *A COURSE IN MIRACLES*.® Gloria and Kenneth Wapnick.
ISBN 0-933291-21-3 • #B-14 • Paperback • 144 pages $8

Available also in Spanish:
LAS PREGUNTAS MAS COMUNES EN TORNO A *UN CURSO EN MILAGROS*
ISBN 0-933291-28-0 • #B-14s • Paperback • 155 pages $8

Available also in German:
DER HIMMEL HAT KEIN GEGENTEIL

Available also in Dutch:
DE MEEST GESTELDA VRAGEN OVER *EEN CURSUS IN WONDEREN*®
Order from: Ankh-Hermes bv • Postbus 125 • 7400 AC Deventer • Netherlands

THE MESSAGE OF *A COURSE IN MIRACLES*.®
Volume One, *All Are Called*.
Volume Two, *Few Choose to Listen*.
Volume One 380 pages; Volume Two 239 pages
ISBN 0-933291-25-6 • #B-15 • Paperback $22 (two-volume set)

Available also in German:
DIE BOTSCHAFT VON *EIN KURS IN WUNDERN*®

THE JOURNEY HOME: "The Obstacles to Peace" in *A Course in Miracles*®
ISBN 0-933291-24-8 • #B-16 • paperback • 510 pages $16.95

Video Tape Albums

(For full descriptions please see our Web site at www.facim.org or call or write for our free catalog)

SEEK NOT TO CHANGE THE COURSE. Reflections on *A Course in Miracles*.®
#V1 • 135 mins. • VHS $30 • PAL (non-U.S.) $40
See also #T16 in Audio Tapes section.

THE REAL WORLD (Three-hour unedited workshop). Gloria and Kenneth Wapnick.
ISBN 0-933291-99-X • #V3 • 3 hrs. • VHS (US) $30 • PAL (non-US) $40.

THE REAL WORLD (Two-hour edited workshop). Gloria and Kenneth Wapnick.
ISBN 0-933291-98-1 • #V4 • 2 hrs. • VHS (US) $20 • PAL (non-US) $30.

AN INTERVIEW WITH KENNETH AND GLORIA WAPNICK. A one-hour interview conducted by Corinne Edwards at the Miracle Network in Chicago in December 1995.
#V5 • 1 hr. • VHS (US) $15 • PAL (non US) $20.

VISIONARIES. This 18-minute video was produced for the PBS series, *Visionaries*, and is narrated by Sam Waterston.
#V6 • 18-min. • VHS (US) $10

THE PATHWAY OF FORGIVENESS.
ISBN 1-59142-008-3 • #V7 • 4 hr. • VHS (US) $30 • PAL (non-U.S.) $40
See also #T64 in Audio Tapes section.

LIVING *A COURSE IN MIRACLES*®
ISBN 1-59142-009-1 • #V8 • two tapes • VHS(US) $30 • PAL(non-U.S.) $40
See also #T67 in Audio Tapes section.

THE MEANING OF THE HOLY INSTANT.
ISBN 1-59142-010-5 • #V9 • two 2-hr. tapes • VHS $20 • PAL (non-U.S.) $3o
See also #T62 in Audio Tapes section.

SPECIAL RELATIONSHIPS: The Home of Guilt.
ISBN 1-59142-012-1 • #V10 • two 2-hr. tapes • VHS $30 • PAL (non-U.S.) $40
See also #T68 in Audio Tapes section.

LOVE AND BE SILENT. King Lear, Defenselessness, and *A Course in Miracles*
ISBN 1-59142-013-X • #V11 • two 2-hr. tapes • VHS $30 • PAL (non-U.S.) $40
See also #T65 in Audio Tapes section.

CLASSES ON THE TEXT OF *A COURSE IN MIRACLES*®.
Introduction • ISBN 1-59142-022-9 • #V12-in • 1 tape • VHS (US) $20
Chapter 1 • ISBN 1-59142-023-7 • #V12-1 • 1 tape • VHS (US) $20
Chapter 2 • ISBN 1-59142-024-5 • #V12-2 • 1 tape • VHS (US) $20
Chapter 3 • ISBN 1-59142-025-3 • #V12-3 • 1 tape • VHS (US) $20
Chapter 4 • ISBN 1-59142-026-1 • #V12-4 • 1 tape • VHS (US) $20
Chapter 5 • ISBN 1-59142-027-X • #V12-5 • 1 tape • VHS (US) $20
Chapter 6 • ISBN 1-59142-028-8 • #V12-6 • 1 tape • VHS (US) $20
Chapter 7 • ISBN 1-59142-029-6 • #V12-7 • 1 tape • VHS (US) $20
Chapter 8 • ISBN 1-59142-030-X • #V12-8 • 1 tape • VHS (US) $20
Chapter 9 • ISBN 1-59142-031-8 • #V12-9 • 1 tape • VHS (US) $20
Chapter 10 • ISBN 1-59142-032-6 • #V12-10 • 1 tape • VHS (US) $20
Chapter 11 • ISBN 1-59142-033-4 • #V12-11 • 1 tape • VHS (US) $20
Chapter 12 • ISBN 1-59142-034-2 • #V12-12 • 1 tape • VHS (US) $20
Chapter 13 • ISBN 1-59142-035-0 • #V12-13 • 1 tape • VHS (US) $20
Chapter 14 • ISBN 1-59142-036-9 • #V12-14 • 1 tape • VHS (US) $20
Chapter 15 • ISBN 1-59142-037-7 • #V12-15 • 1 tape • VHS (US) $20
Chapter 16 • ISBN 1-59142-038-5 • #V12-16 • 1 tape • VHS (US) $20
Chapter 17 • ISBN 1-59142-039-3 • #V12-17 • 1 tape • VHS (US) $20
Chapter 18 • ISBN 1-59142-040-7 • #V12-18 • 1 tape • VHS (US) $20
Chapter 19 • ISBN 1-59142-041-5 • #V12-19 • 1 tape • VHS (US) $20
Chapter 20 • ISBN 1-59142-042-3 • #V12-20 • 1 tape • VHS (US) $20
Chapter 21 • ISBN 1-59142-043-1 • #V12-21 • 1 tape • VHS (US) $20
Chapter 22 • ISBN 1-59142-044-X • #V12-22 • 1 tape • VHS (US) $20
Chapter 23 • ISBN 1-59142-045-8 • #V12-23 • 1 tape • VHS (US) $20
Chapter 24 • ISBN 1-59142-046-6 • #V12-24 • 1 tape • VHS (US) $20
Chapter 25 • ISBN 1-59142-047-4 • #V12-25 • 1 tape • VHS (US) $20
Chapter 26 • ISBN 1-59142-048-2 • #V12-26 • 1 tape • VHS (US) $20
Chapter 27 • ISBN 1-59142-049-0 • #V12-27 • 1 tape • VHS (US) $20
Chapter 28 • ISBN 1-59142-050-4 • #V12-28 • 1 tape • VHS (US) $20
Chapter 29 • ISBN 1-59142-051-2 • #V12-29 • 1 tape • VHS (US) $20
Chapter 30 • ISBN 1-59142-052-0 • #V12-30 • 1 tape • VHS (US) $20
Chapter 31 • ISBN 1-59142-053-9 • #V12-31 • 1 tape • VHS (US) $20
See also #T61-1 through T61-8 in Audio Tapes section.
See also #CD61-1 through CD61-8 in Audio Compact Discs section.

JUSTICE RETURNED TO LOVE.
ISBN 1-59142-054-7 • #V13 • two 2-hr. tapes • VHS (US) $30
See also #T81 in Audio Tapes section.

THE TIME MACHINE.
ISBN 1-59142-055-5 • #V14 • two 2-hr. tapes • VHS (US) $30
See also #T73 in Audio Tapes section.

FORGIVENESS AND THE END OF TIME.
ISBN 1-59142-067-9 • #V15 • two 2-hr. tapes • VHS (US) $30
See also #T74 in Audio Tapes section.

FROM DARKNESS TO LIGHT.
ISBN 1-59142-068-7 • #V16 • two 2-hr. tapes • VHS (US) $30
See also #T63 in Audio Tapes section.

JESUS: Symbol And Reality.
ISBN 1-59142-069-5 • #V17 • two 2-hr. tapes • VHS (US) $30
See also #T66 in Audio Tapes section.

DREAMING THE DREAM.
ISBN 1-59142-070-9 • #V18 • two 2-hr. tapes • VHS (US) $30
See also #T69 in Audio Tapes section.

THE COMPASSION OF THE MIRACLE.
ISBN 1-59142-071-7 • #V19 • two 2-hr. tapes • VHS (US) $30
See also #T70 in Audio Tapes section.

HEALING THE DREAM OF SICKNESS.
ISBN 1-59142-072-5 • #V20 • two 2-hr. tapes • VHS (US) $30
See also #T75 in Audio Tapes section.

THE CHANGELESS DWELLING PLACE.
ISBN 1-59142-077-6 • #V21 • two 2-hr. tapes • VHS (US) $30
See also #T76 in Audio Tapes section.

TO BE OR NOT TO BE: Hamlet, Death, and *A Course in Miracles.*®
ISBN 1-59142-079-2 • #V22 • two 2-hr. tapes • VHS (US) $30
See also #T77 in Audio Tapes section.

FORM vs. CONTENT: Sex and Money.
ISBN 1-59142-080-6 • #V23 • two 2-hr. tapes • VHS (US) $30
See also #T78 in Audio Tapes section.

THE PRODIGAL SON.
ISBN 1-59142-081-4 • #V24 • two 2-hr. tapes • VHS (US) $30
See also #T79 in Audio Tapes section.

THE PROBLEM OF EVIL.
ISBN 1-59142-095-4 • #V25 • two 2-hr. tapes • VHS (US) $30
See also #T82 in Audio Tapes section.

CLASSES ON THE MANUAL FOR TEACHERS OF *A COURSE IN MIRACLES.*®
Vol. 1 • Introduction; Sections 1–3 • ISBN 1-59142-085-7 • #V26-1 • 1 tape • VHS (US)$20
Vol. 2 • Section 4 • ISBN 1-59142-086-5 • #V26-2 • 1 tape • VHS (US)$20
Vol, 3 • Sections 5–8 • ISBN 1-59142-087-3 • #V26-3 • 1 tape • VHS (US)$20
Vol. 4 • Sections 9–13 • ISBN 1-59142-088-1 • #V26-4 • 1 tape • VHS (US)$20
Vol. 5 • Sections 14–17 • ISBN 1-59142-089-X • #V26-5 • 1 tape • VHS (US)$20
Vol. 6 • Sections 18–21 • ISBN 1-59142-090-3 • #V26-6 • 1 tape • VHS (US)$20
Vol. 7 • Sections 22–25 • ISBN 1-59142-091-1 • #V26-7 • 1 tape • VHS (US)$20
Vol. 8 • Sections 26–29 • ISBN 1-59142-0092-X • #V26-8 • 1 tape • VHS (US)$20
Vol. 9 • Clarification of Terms, Part 1 • ISBN 1-59142-093-8 • #V26-9 • 1 tape • VHS (US)$20
Vol. 10 • Clarification of Terms, Part 2 • ISBN 1-59142-094-6 • #V26-10 • 1 tape • VHS (US)$20
See also #T83-1 and T83-2 in Audio Tapes section.
See also #CD83-1 and CD83-2 in Audio Compact Discs section.

THE QUALITY OF MERCY.
ISBN 1-59142-099-7 • #V27 • two 2-hr. tapes • VHS (US) $30
See also #T84 in Audio Tapes section.

A TALE TOLD BY AN IDIOT: Macbeth, Guilt, and *A Course in Miracles.*®
ISBN 1-59142-102-0 • #V28 • two 2-hr. tapes • VHS (US) $30
See also #T85 in Audio Tapes section.

HEALING: Hearing the Melody
ISBN 1-59142-112-8 • #V29 • two 2-hr. tapes • VHS (US) $30
See also #T88 in the Audio Tapes section.
See also #CD88 in the Audio Compact Discs section.

LOVING NOT WISELY BUT TOO WELL: Othello, Specialness and *A Course in Miracles.*®
ISBN 1-59142-131-4 • #V30 • two 2-hr. tapes • VHS (US) $30
See also #T90 in the Audio Tapes section.
See also #CD90 in the Audio Compact Discs section.

AN INTRODUCTION TO *A COURSE IN MIRACLES*
ISBN 1-59142-133-0 • #V31 • one 98 min. tape • VHS (US) #10

Audio Tapes and Compact Discs

Classes and Workshops

(For full descriptions please see our Web site at www.facim.org or call or write for our free catalog)

CHRISTIAN PSYCHOLOGY IN *A COURSE IN MIRACLES*.® Audio version of the second edition of the book, read by Kenneth Wapnick.
Tapes: ISBN 0-933291-50-7 • #T2 • 2 tapes $10

THE SIMPLICITY OF SALVATION.
Tapes: ISBN 0-933291-51-5 • #T1 • 8 tapes $48

ATONEMENT WITHOUT SACRIFICE: Christianity, the Bible, and the Course.
Tapes: ISBN 0-933291-53-1 • #T3 • 2 tapes $10

THE EGO AND FORGIVENESS. Introductory overview of the Course.
Tapes: ISBN 0-933291-55-8 • #T5 • 2 tapes $10
Available also in German:
DAS EGO UND DIE VERGEBUNG

SPECIAL RELATIONSHIPS—PART 1.
Tapes: ISBN 0-933291-59-0 • #T9 • 8 tapes $48

SPECIAL RELATIONSHIPS—PART 2.
Tapes: ISBN 0-933291-60-4 • #T10 • 6 tapes $36

CAUSE AND EFFECT.
Tapes: ISBN 0-933291-63-9 • #T13 • 8 tapes $48

THE GIFTS OF GOD. A discussion of the inspired poetry of Helen Schucman.
Tapes: ISBN 0-933291-65-5 • #T15 • 3 tapes $18

SEEK NOT TO CHANGE THE COURSE: Reflections on *A Course in Miracles*.® Gloria and Kenneth Wapnick. Audio version of video tape of the same name.
Tapes: ISBN 0-933291-66-3 • #T16 • 2 tapes $10

LOVE DOES NOT OPPOSE. Gloria and Kenneth Wapnick.
Tapes: ISBN 0-933291-67-1 • #T17 • 8 tapes $48

THE SONG OF PRAYER.
Tapes: ISBN 0-933291-68-X • #T18 • 10 tapes $60

THE ORIGIN OF *A COURSE IN MIRACLES*.®
Tapes: ISBN 0-933291-69-8 • #T19 • 1 tape $6

I WILL BE STILL AN INSTANT AND GO HOME.
Tapes: ISBN 0-933291-70-1 • #T20 • 1 tape $6

JESUS: Teacher of Forgiveness • Model of Resurrection.
Tapes: ISBN 0-933291-71-X • #T21 • 8 tapes $48

THE AUTHORITY PROBLEM.
Tapes: ISBN 0-933291-72-8 • #T22 • 5 tapes $30

OUR GRATITUDE TO GOD.
Tapes: ISBN 0-933291-73-6 • #T23 • 5 tapes $30

SICKNESS AND HEALING.
Tapes: ISBN 0-933291-74-4 • #T24 • 8 tapes $48

WHAT IT MEANS TO BE A TEACHER OF GOD.
Tapes: ISBN 0-933291-75-2 • #T25 • 6 tapes $36

OVEREATING: A Dialogue. An Application of the Principles of
A COURSE IN MIRACLES.®
Tapes: ISBN 0-933291-76-0 • #T26 • 1 tape $6

TO JUDGE OR NOT TO JUDGE.
Tapes: ISBN 0-933291-77-9 • #T27 • 4 tapes $24

HEALING THE UNHEALED HEALER.
Tapes: ISBN 0-933291-78-7 • #T28 • 8 tapes $48

THE REAL WORLD: Our Home away from Home.
Tapes: ISBN 0-933291-79-5 • #T29 • 8 tapes $48

TRUE EMPATHY: The Greater Joining.
Tapes: ISBN 0-933291-80-9 • #T30 • 8 tapes $48

JESUS: The Manifestation of the Holy Spirit.
Tapes: ISBN 0-933291-81-7 • #T31 • 5 tapes $30

THE LAWS OF CHAOS: Our War with God.
Tapes: ISBN 0-933291-82-5 • #T32 • 12 tapes $72

"THERE MUST BE ANOTHER WAY."
Tapes: ISBN 0-933291-83-3 • #T33 • 1 tape $6
Available also in German:
ES MUSS EINEN ANDEREN WEG GEBEN

THE METAPHYSICS OF SEPARATION AND FORGIVENESS.
Tapes: ISBN 0-933291-84-1 • #T34 • 1 tape $6
Available also in German:
DIE METAPHYSIK DER TRENNUNG UND VERGEBUNG

THE WORKBOOK OF *A COURSE IN MIRACLES*:® Its Place in the
Curriculum —Theory And Practice.
Tapes: ISBN 0-933291-85-X • #T35 • 8 tapes $48

MAKING THE HOLY SPIRIT SPECIAL: The Arrogance of the Ego.
Tapes: ISBN 0-933291-86-8 • #T36 • 7 tapes $42

THE MEANING OF JUDGMENT.
Tapes: ISBN 0-933291-87-6 • #T37 • 1 tape $6

THE WEB OF SPECIALNESS.
Tapes: ISBN 0-933291-88-4 • #T38 • 12 tapes $72

DUALITY AS METAPHOR IN *A COURSE IN MIRACLES*.®
Tapes: ISBN 0-933291-89-2 • #T39 • 8 tapes $48

RULES FOR DECISION.
Tapes: ISBN 0-933291-90-6 • #T40 • 8 tapes $48

I WANT THE PEACE OF GOD.
Tapes: ISBN 0-933291-91-4 • #T41 • 1 tape $6
Available also in German:
ICH WILL DEN FRIEDEN GOTTES

FORGIVING JESUS: "Stranger on the Road."
Tapes: ISBN 0-933291-92-2 • #T42 • 2 tapes $10

THE BIBLE FROM THE PERSPECTIVE OF *A COURSE IN MIRACLES*.®
Kenneth and Gloria Wapnick.
Tapes: ISBN 0-933291-93-0 • #T43 • 6 tapes $36

THE THEOLOGY OF *A COURSE IN MIRACLES*.® Kenneth and Gloria Wapnick.
Tapes: ISBN 0-933291-94-9 • #T44 • 2 tapes $10

THE INHERITANCE OF GOD'S SON. Kenneth and Gloria Wapnick.
Tapes: ISBN 0-933291-95-7 • #T45 • 2 tapes $10

THE SIGN OF CHRISTMAS IS A STAR. Kenneth and Gloria Wapnick.
Tapes: ISBN 0-933291-96-5 • #T46 • 2 tapes $10

THE HOLY CHRIST IS BORN IN ME TODAY. Kenneth and Gloria Wapnick.
Tapes: ISBN 0-933291-97-3 • #T47 • 2 tapes $10

FROM TIME TO TIMELESSNESS.
Tapes: ISBN 0-933291-49-3 • #T48 • 1 tape $6

CLIMBING THE LADDER HOME.
Tapes: ISBN 0-933291-48-5 • #T49 • 5 tapes $30

HOW WILL THE WORLD END?
Tapes: ISBN 0-933291-47-7 • #T50 • 2 tapes $10

THE IMPORTANCE OF JESUS.
Tapes: ISBN 0-933291-46-9 • #T51 • 2 tapes $10

LEARNING FROM THE HOLY SPIRIT: A Commentary on Lesson 193: "All things are lessons God would have me learn."
Tapes: ISBN 0-933291-46-0 • #T52 • 2 tapes $10

THE MEANING OF FORGIVENESS.
Tapes: ISBN 0-933291-44-2 • #T53 • 2 tapes $10
CDs: ISBN 1-59142-106-3 • #CD53 • 2 CDs $15

THE KINDNESS OF HEALING.
Tapes: ISBN 0-933291-43-4 • #T54 • 1 tape $6
CD: ISBN 1-59142-115-2 • #CD54 • 2 CDs $15

THE GIFT OF THE EGO: FEAR – THE GIFT OF GOD: LOVE.
Tapes: ISBN 0-933291-42-6 • #T55 • 8 tapes $48

THE EXPERIENCE OF *A COURSE IN MIRACLES*®. A Commentary on "Development of Trust" (manual for teachers).
Tapes: ISBN 0-933291- 41-8 • #T56 • 8 tapes $48

SEPARATION AND FORGIVENESS: The Four Splits and Their Undoing.
Tapes: ISBN 0-933291-40-X • #T57 • 7 tapes $42

THE WORKBOOK LESSONS OF *A COURSE IN MIRACLES*®:
Tapes:
Vol. I • ISBN 0-933291-38-8 • #T58-1 • 8 tapes $32
Vol. II • ISBN 0-933291-32-9 • #T58-2 • 10 tapes $49
Vol. III • ISBN 0-933291-33-7 • #T58-3 • 11 tapes $49

THE WORKBOOK LESSONS OF *A COURSE IN MIRACLES®*: (cont.)
Tapes (cont.):
Vol. IV • ISBN 0-933291-34-5 • #T58-4 • 8 tapes $32
Vol. V • ISBN 0-933291-35-3 • #T58-5 • 8 tapes $32
Vol. VI • ISBN 0-933291-36-1 • #T58-6 • 10 tapes $40
CDs:
Vol. I • ISBN 1-59142-120-9 • #CD58-1 • 7 discs $40
Vol. II • ISBN 1-59142-121-7 • #CD58-2 • 5 discs $30
Vol. III • ISBN 1-59142-122-5 • #CD58-3 • 5 discs $30
Vol. IV • ISBN 1-59142-123-3 • #CD58-4 • 12 discs $65
Vol. V • ISBN 1-59142-124-1 • #CD58-5 • 8 discs $45
Vol. VI • ISBN 1-59142-125-X • #CD58-6 • 9 discs $50
Vol. VII • ISBN 1-59142-126-8 • #CD58-7 • 10 discs $55

THE QUIET ANSWER: Asking the Holy Spirit.
Tapes: ISBN 0-933291-37-X • #T59 • 3 tapes $18

THE OBSTACLES TO PEACE.
Tapes: ISBN 0-933291-31-0 • #T60 • 8 tapes $48

CLASSES ON THE TEXT OF *A COURSE IN MIRACLES®:*
Tapes:
Vol. I • ISBN 1-59142-000-8 • #T61-1 • 8 tapes $32
Vol. II • ISBN 1-59142-001-6 • #T61-2 • 8 tapes $32
Vol. III • ISBN 1-59142-002-4 • #T61-3 • 8 tapes $32
Vol. IV • ISBN 1-59142-003-2 • #T61-4 • 8 tapes $32
Vol. V • ISBN 1-59142-004-0 • #T61-5 • 8 tapes $32
Vol. VI • ISBN 1-59142-005-9 • #T61-6 • 8 tapes $32
Vol. VII • ISBN 1-59142-006-7 • #T61-7 • 8 tapes $32
Vol. VIII • ISBN 1-59142-007-5 • #T61-8 • 8 tapes $32
CDs:
Vol. I • ISBN 1-59142-059-8 • #CD61-1 • 8 tapes $32
Vol. II • ISBN 1-59142-060-1 • #CD61-2 • 8 tapes $32
Vol. III • ISBN 1-59142-061-X • #CD61-3 • 8 tapes $32
Vol. IV • ISBN 1-59142-062-8 • #CD61-4 • 8 tapes $32
Vol. V • ISBN 1-59142-063-6 • #CD61-5 • 8 tapes $32
Vol. VI • ISBN 1-59142-064-4 • #CD61-6 • 8 tapes $32
Vol. VII • ISBN 1-59142-065-2 • #CD61-7 • 8 tapes $32
Vol. VIII • ISBN 1-59142-066-0 • #CD61-8 • 8 tapes $32
See also #V12-in. throughV12-31 in Video Tapes section.

THE MEANING OF THE HOLY INSTANT.
Tapes: ISBN 1-59142-011-3 • #T62 • 2 tapes $10
See also #V9 in Video Tapes section.

FROM DARKNESS TO LIGHT.
Tapes: ISBN 1-59142-014-8 • #T63 • 4 tapes $20
See also #V16 in Video Tapes section.

THE PATHWAY OF FORGIVENESS.
Tapes: ISBN 1-59142-008-3• #T64 • 4 tapes $20
See also #V7 in Video Tapes section.

LOVE AND BE SILENT: King Lear, Defenselessness, and *A Course in Miracles.*®
Tapes: ISBN 1-59142-016-4 • #T65 • 4 tapes $20
See also #V11 in Video Tapes section.

JESUS: Symbol and Reality.
Tapes: ISBN 1-59142-017-2 • #T66 • 4 tapes $20
See also #V17 in Video Tapes section.

LIVING *A COURSE IN MIRACLES*®.
Tapes: ISBN 1-59142-018-0 • #T67 • 4 tapes $20
See also #V8 in Video Tapes section.

SPECIAL RELATIONSHIPS: The Home of Guilt.
Tapes: ISBN 1-59142-019-9 • #T68 • 4 tapes $20
See also #V10 in Video Tapes section.

DREAMING THE DREAM.
Tapes: ISBN 1-59142-020-2 • #T69 • 4 tapes $20
See also #V18 in Video Tapes section.

THE COMPASSION OF THE MIRACLE.
Tapes: ISBN 1-59142-021-0 • #T70 • 4 tapes $20
See also #V19 in Video Tapes section.

APPROACHING *A COURSE IN MIRACLES*®: A Commentary on Lesson 188: "The peace of God is shining in me now."
Tapes: ISBN 1-59142-056-3 • #T71 • 1 tape $5

AN OVERVIEW OF *A COURSE IN MIRACLES*®.
Tapes: ISBN 1-59142-057-1 • #T72 • 1 tape $6

THE TIME MACHINE.
Tapes: ISBN 1-59142-058-X • #T73 • 4 tapes $20
See also #V14 in Video Tapes section.

FORGIVENESS AND THE END OF TIME.
Tapes: ISBN 1-59142-073-3 • #T74 • 4 tapes $20
See also #V15 in Video Tapes section.

HEALING THE DREAM OF SICKNESS.
Tapes: ISBN 1-59142-074-1 • #T75 • 4 tapes $20
See also #V20 in Video Tapes section.

THE CHANGELESS DWELLING PLACE.
Tapes: ISBN 1-59142-075-X • #T76 • 4 tapes $20
See also #V21 in Video Tapes section.

TO BE OR NOT TO BE: Hamlet, Death, and *A Course in Miracles.*®
Tapes: ISBN 1-59142-076-8 • #T77 • 4 tapes $20
See also #V22 in Video Tapes section.

FORM vs. CONTENT: Sex and Money.
Tapes: ISBN 1-59142-078-4 • #T78 • 4 tapes $20
See also #V23 in Video Tapes section.

THE PRODIGAL SON.
Tapes: ISBN 1-59142-082-2 • #T79 • 4 tapes $20
See also #V24 in Video Tapes section.

RETURNING HOME.
Tapes: ISBN 1-59142-083-0 • #T80 • 4 tapes $20

JUSTICE RETURNED TO LOVE.
Tapes: ISBN 1-59142-084-9 • #T81 • 4 tapes $20
See also #V13 in Video Tapes section.

THE PROBLEM OF EVIL
Tapes: ISBN 1-59142-096-2 • #T82 • 4 tapes $20
See also #V25 in Video Tapes section.

CLASSES ON THE MANUAL FOR TEACHERS OF *A COURSE IN MIRACLES®*
Tapes:
Vol. 1 • ISBN 1-59142-097-0 • #T83-1 • 10 tapes • $55
Vol. 1 • ISBN 1-59142-098-9 • #T83-2 • 10 tapes • $55
CDs:
Vol. 1 • ISBN 1-59142-107-1 • #CD83-1 • 10 CDs • $55
Vol. 1 • ISBN 1-59142-108-X • #CD83-2 • 10 CDs • $55
See also #V29 in the Video Tapes section.

THE QUALITY OF MERCY
Tapes: ISBN 1-59142-100-4 • #T84 • 4 tapes $20
See also #V27 in Video Tapes section.

A TALE TOLD BY AN IDIOT: Macbeth, Guilt, and *A Course in Miracles®*
Tapes: ISBN 1-59142-101-2 • #T85 • 4 tapes $20
See also #V28 in Video Tapes section.

THE JOURNEY: From the Ego Self to the True Self
Tapes: ISBN 1-59142-104-7 • #T86 • 12 tapes $60
CDs: ISBN 1-59142-103-9 • #CD86 • 16 CDs $85

LIVING IN THE WORLD: Prison or Classroom
Tapes: ISBN 1-59142-110-1 • #T87 • 8 tapes $40
CDs: ISBN 1-59142-105-5 • #CD87 • 8 CDs $45

HEALING: Hearing the Melody
Tapes: ISBN 1-59142-111-X • #T88 • 4 tapes $20
CDs: ISBN 1-59142-109-8 • #CD88 • 4 CDs $25
See also #V29 in the Video Tapes section.

DECIDING FOR GOD
Tapes: ISBN 1-59142-114-4 • #T89 • 2 tapes $10
CDs: ISBN 1-59142-113-6 • #CD89 • 2 CDs $15

LOVING NOT WISELY BUT TOO WELL: Othello, Specialness and *A Course In Miracles.*®
Tapes: ISBN 1-59142-117-9 • #T90 • 4 tapes $20
CDs: ISBN 1-59142-117-9 • #CD90 • 4 CDs $20
See also #V29 in the Video Tapes section.

JESUS: Light in the Dream
Tapes: ISBN 1-59142-119-5 • #T91 • 2 tapes $10
CDs: ISBN 1-59142-118-7 • #CD91 • 2 CDs $15

LETTING GO OF JUDGMENT: Entering the Stately Calm Within
Tapes: ISBN 1-59142-128-4 • #T92 • 4 tapes $20
CDs: ISBN 1-59142-127-6 • #CD92 • 3 CDs $20

PSYCHOTHERAPY: PURPOSE, PROCESS AND PRACTICE.
A Commentary on the Pamphlet
Tapes: ISBN 1-59142-130-6 • #T93 • 8 tapes $40
CDs: ISBN 1-59142-129-2 • #CD93 • 8 CDs $45

See next page for ordering information

Ordering Information

For orders ***in the continental U.S. only***, please add $6.00 for the first item, and $1.00 for each additional item, for shipping and handling.

For orders to ***all other countries*** (SURFACE MAIL), and to ***Alaska, Hawaii***, and ***Puerto Rico*** (FIRST CLASS MAIL), please add $6.00 for the first item and $2.00 for each additional item.

California State residents please add local sales tax.

VISA, MasterCard, Discover, American Express accepted.

Order from:

Foundation for *A Course in Miracles*®
Dept. B
41397 Buecking Drive
Temecula, CA 92590
(909) 296-6261 • FAX (909) 296-5455
or

visit our Web site at *www.facim.org*

* * * * *

A COURSE IN MIRACLES and other scribed material
may be ordered from:

Foundation for Inner Peace
P.O. Box 598
Mill Valley, CA 94942
(415) 388-2060

A COURSE IN MIRACLES, Second edition (softcover): $30
A COURSE IN MIRACLES, Complete edition (paperback): $20

PSYCHOTHERAPY: PURPOSE, PROCESS AND PRACTICE: $5
THE SONG OF PRAYER: PRAYER, FORGIVENESS, HEALING: $5
THE GIFTS OF GOD: $21
CONCORDANCE OF *A COURSE IN MIRACLES*®: $49.95